The Flour is Different

Das Mehl ist Anders

German Heritage Recipes and Traditions

by Trudy Gilgenast

With Illustrations by Kathryn S. Dodson

The Middle Atlantic Press
848 Church Street
Wilmington, Delaware 19899

Reprinted by arrangement with the author

ISBN: 0-912608-34-4
Printed in the United States of America

Fourth Middle Atlantic Press Printing February 1995

The Middle Atlantic Press, Inc.
848 Church Street, P.O. Box 1948
Wilmington, Delaware 19899

Library of Congress Catalog Number 8261839

Table of Contents

Proverbs and Sayings 4

Dedication 5

Introduction 6

Blessings 9

Good luck 10

Was gibt es zu essen? (Sample meals) 11

Silvester und Neujahr (New Year's Eve and New Year) 13

Fasching (Carnival and Lent) 26

Ostern (Easter) 40

Himmelfahrt, Pfingsten, Tag der Arbeit
   (Ascension, Pentecost, Labor Day and Hot Summer Days 52

Herbst Feste (Autumn) 84

Sankt Martinstag (Saint Martin's Day) 116

Advent, Sankt Nikolaus, Weihnachten
   (Advent, Saint Nicholas, Christmas) 136

Proverbs and Sayings

The Germans are known for their proverbs and witty sayings and much of their humor is peppered with satire, wisdom and folkloric imagery. They 'salt it away' so to speak and produce an appropriate maxim at the most propitious moment. Through the daily activities and especially through their celebrations the Germans display a tremendous sense of enthusiasm and a zest for life. They are rather tenacious of their heritage, social customs and principles of living. Maxims such as 'Arbeit macht das Leben süss' (work makes life sweet) are sprinkled throughout their culture and appear to be markers throughout the year and their lives to which they adhere.

Various sayings have to do with food or eating:

Wir leben nicht, um zu essen
Wir essen, um zu leben
 (We don't live to eat; we eat to live) Socrates

Hunger ist der beste Koch
 (Hunger is the best cook)

Man ist, was man isst!
 (One is that which one eats!)

Die Liebe geht durch den Magen.
 (Love goes through the stomach)

Morgens wie ein Edelmann
Mittags wie ein Bauersmann
Abends wie ein Bettelmann
Und du bleibst gesund!
 (Mornings like a nobleman
 midday like a plowman
 evenings like a beggarman
 and you remain healthy!)

4

I dedicate this book
to my dear parents
Elly and Alfred Gilgenast;
their love and inspiration
have made my life richer
by enabling me to experience
the
'best of two worlds'!

Introduction

Today's German cuisine is as varied and international as American cooking, for there is a ready availability of all sorts of fresh vegetables and ingredients to whet the appetite of every palate. Housewives on both sides of the ocean are usually very busy and the image of the German housewife who spends hours in the kitchen is a myth today. Although many recipes still require time to prepare, the introduction of convenience food items offers shortcuts. I have found, however, that everyone has a special craving now and then to eat a meal or dish 'just like the one my mother used to make' or one that comes from 'my home area' and brings back memories of old traditions. These foods with their traditions provide a vital link between generations and I have tried to preserve this aspect of the German heritage through a collection of personal 'Lieblingsrezepte' (favorite recipes) along with a brief description of festivals celebrated through the calendar year. For many of these ethnic cooks the saying 'die Liebe geht durch den Magen' (love goes through the stomach) illustrates their genuine devotion in taking the time to prepare foods that are both attractive and pleasing.

The recipes, shared by German-Americans primarily in the Delaware Valley area, have, in numerous instances, been passed along from mother to daughter to granddaughter and even great-granddaughter! These contributions illustrate an acculturation in the culinary arts, a preserving of an aspect of the German culture. This group is a sampling of other German clusters found throughout the United States; in some areas the German influence is greater, in others, less. Food is, nevertheless, a basic expression of the culture and a link with traditions. It is not only that cohesive ingredient linking generations within a culture but also the thread which crosses all cultures. Foods offer a commonality of expression.

In adapting to the new environs the German-American housewife often found that recipes turned out differently from those prepared in the homeland. Often with dismay she exclaimed: "Ach, das Mehl ist anders" (the flour is different). Indeed she discovered differences in ingredients as well as in measurements!

Reflecting the assorted culinary customs practiced by the diverse group of cooks both male and female, contributing to this book, the recipe styles are varied. Some are detailed, some free-form; a few are in German as well as in English and there are several that can best be described as following the pinch-of-this style, prevalent among German cooks.

The recipes are presented with the American measurements first with metric equivalents (when indicated) in parentheses. Generally, the flour, sugar and solids (butter, cheese, etc.) have been converted as is the custom, to metric weights. Tablespoon and teaspoon measures have been left unconverted because of the closeness between the two systems.

For other items, metric volume conversions, sometimes in addition to metric weight, are used because this is what the American cook is accustomed to. Also, metric volume conversions have been commonly available on measuring utensils sold in the U.S. for some time.

According to Betty Crocker's International Cookbook, when the U.S. converts totally to metric measure, not expected for at least ten years, measuring will continue to be by volume, not by weight, and there will be metric measuring utensils available to match the metric recipes.

The recipes also reflect favorite and traditional dishes from most regions of Germany. Holidays, especially Easter and Christmas, are an important aspect of family life and are times for special food preparations and baking. The inclusion of several versions of one type recipe authenticates variety as to region or family. The north German cuisine reflects more the use of potatoes, whereas the south employs more flour dishes such as dumplings and noodles. Christmas baked goods also vary slightly from kitchen to kitchen and from region to region. The recipes are shared with the common bond of preserving and cultivating customs so that future generations will continue to enjoy these foods.

As you read through the brief description of each festival, keep in mind that the German immigrant has kept alive more vividly some of these traditions and customs in his adopted environs than might be observed in the homeland. A feeling of security in being with those of one's own background is prevalent in most ethnic groups. German families enjoy getting together for birthdays, weddings, confirmation and first communions or whatever the occasion for a celebration. They claim 'Man soll die Feste feiern wie sie fallen' (one should celebrate the festivals as they occur). Some families enjoy hiking together or meeting to sing folk songs or rounds. Others meet to engage in creative projects for gifts or decorations especially at Easter and Christmas.

Friends get together in homes for coffee and cake and enjoy the opportunity to chat in the mother tongue. They feel the need and importance of keeping up their language proficiency. Many express disappointment that their children usually do not have the opportunity to learn the language formally at an early age in school, even though they hear it spoken at home. This is another important link of communication between generations and cultures which contributes to the preservation of one's heritage.

Other friends prefer to gather socially to play cards, others form a book club and discuss new German books, and still others prefer to attend local German films, theaters and concerts. Tradition for some is the 'Frühschoppen', a glass of wine with bread and cheese, after church or a 'Bowle', a punch served while visiting in the evening and talking with friends. Sports, folk and social dancing, and choral singing are other activities enjoyed through the local German-American Club. Whatever the activity you can be sure there is an abundance of good food. The great variety of these foods demonstrates a versatility in the culinary arts of the people.

This book has evolved from my interest in the German heritage and from research and oral history undertaken during a sabbatical semester. Primarily through personal interviews of local German-Americans I have investigated and recorded their accounts of customs, traditions and authentic recipes which reflect an important expression of their cultural identity. I myself grew up experiencing a bicultural heritage and have long remembered celebrations with aromas of special foods and baked goods wafting from my mother's kitchen. My father, brother and I all helped with the meticulous preparation of mother's most sought after speciality, the Christmas Stollen. These memories and the reminiscences of members of the German-American community serve to unwind the past and express a cultural link with the present. The culinary arts represent an important expression of the rich legacy which the Germans have woven into local life.

Gathering these recipes has been an exciting experience because I have met and worked with so many wonderful and interested people. I extend thanks to many but especially to those people who generously shared their recipes to be included in the collection. Their names are signed with the recipes submitted. Many others offered valuable information through personal interviews. I am especially grateful to the following: Hilde Cox, for enthusiastically sharing her cultural heritage; Annelies Menta, for her hours of typing and transcribing; Lise Monty, foods' writer, for her publicity and tremendous help in conversions of measurements; Nancy Sawin, for her generous support in publishing the book; and finally to my dear high school friend, Kathryn Dodson, for her lovely illustrations and untiring encouragement.

May all of you who read and experiment with these recipes learn to enjoy and treasure favorite German customs, foods and traditions!

SITT' UND BRAUCH DER ALTEN, WOLLEN WIR ERHALTEN!
(We want to preserve the customs and traditions of old!)

Trudy Gilgenast

Blessings

Before and after meals

GESEGNETE MAHLZEIT
(Blessed Meal)

Erika Schirm

This custom is carried over from my aunt who was born in Germany and married and raised a family in upstate New York:

Whenever we have company for dinner, after the head of the household (the father) says grace, we make a circle by holding hands with the persons sitting at our right and left, and wish each other a "Gesegnete Mahlzeit" (blessed meal).

TISCHGEBET
(Grace)

Brigitte Conrad

In our family we usually pray **after** dinner. We say, "Wir danken Dir Herr Jesus Christ, dass Du unser Gast gewesen bist." (We thank you, Lord Jesus, that you were our guest). Then we turn to each other extending our hands to make a circle and mother or father says, "Gesegnete Mahlzeit" (blessed meal). Everyone responds: "Gesegnete Mahlzeit". Only after giving this sign is everyone excused.

Good Luck

Good luck symbols appear throughout the year, but especially at Christmas and New Year when you wish luck and happiness for the next year. The chimney sweep is a popular figure all year. If you see one while walking along the street, you should go over to him to shake hands or just to touch him! (He expects it and is usually good-natured about his position as a bearer of good luck. In recent times, however, there are also female chimney sweeps!)

Other symbols include the four-leaf clover, the red-white mushroom and the little pig. 'Schwein haben' means that you are lucky. This saying is derived from a German card game of the 16th century. On the highest card, the ace, there was a picture of a pig, for the ace was called 'Daus' or 'Sau'. Thus, the holder of the ace held the lucky card.

WAS GIBT ES ZU ESSEN?
(Sample meals)

FRÜHSTUCK
(Breakfast)

Rolls	*Optional:*
Butter, marmalade	Black or rye bread
Coffee	Assorted cold cuts; sausages
Milk or cocoa	Eggs - soft or hard boiled

MITTAGESSEN
(Noon meal)

A hot meal or dinner is usually served between 11:30 a.m. and 2:00 p.m. Often no beverage is taken with the meal; however, beer, wine or non-alcoholic beverages are popular. Coffee is usually not served, but taken later in the afternoon.

Meatless meals

1. Soup - any variety including some meat or wurst (added for taste)

2. Pancake or flour-base meal; assorted cooked fruit preserves or compotes.

3. Egg dishes

Sunday dinner

Rouladen	Dessert:
Dumplings	Pudding or
Red cabbage	fruit compote

Warmer days

Potato salad	Dessert:
Chicken (hot or cold)	Pudding or
Salad - lettuce or cucumber	fruit compote

KAFFEE KLATSCH
(Coffee get together)

The coffee hour occurs at 3:00 or 4:00 p.m. and is an institution amongst the Germans. The coffee table is set with very special care. A beautifully-embroidered tablecloth, fine china and cut flowers adorn the table. The love of beauty is reflected in the entire table decoration, for this should be attractive to the eye as well as to the stomach! A variety of cakes and tortes served with whipped-cream are available in the Cafe-Konditorei; when invited to someone's home at least two culinary delights are offered. Most important of all is a good strong filter-type cup of coffee. Many hostesses grind their own coffee to insure the utmost of freshness.

ABENDESSEN
(Supper)

At supper beer or wine, or on colder days, a hot drink is enjoyed. Coffee is usually available in restaurants after the coffee hour; however, a variety of herb teas is popular.

Breads for open-faced sandwiches
Assorted cold cuts (Aufschnitt) or meat salads
Cheeses
Tomatoes
Beverages

Platter of appetizers

Such a platter may be served to guests at an evening get-together or for special occasions.

Cheeses or pumpernickel
Salmon garnished with egg slices
Cheese, ham and tongue open-faced sandwiches garnished with pickle or cucumber slices or salmon
Egg sandwiches decorated with mayonnaise, anchovies and capers
Radishes with cress, chives or anchovies
Russian eggs

Wurst varieties

Many sausages and wursts are available for all tastes. The following suggests a small list and offers the reader an adventure of discovery. Local delis usually offer these as well as a variety of other meat delights.

Bratwurst	Leberwurst (fein; grob)
Weisswurst	Landjäger
Knackwurst	Schwartenmagen
Salami	Zungenwurst
Bauernschinken	Leberkäse
Teewurst	Schinkenwurst
Mettwurst	Fleischwurst
Blutwurst	

SILVESTER UND NEUJAHR
(New Year's Eve and New Year)

The last day of the year is referred to as 'Silvester' named after Pope Silvester I (314-335), the Roman-Catholic saint of December 31. The celebrations on this day are similar to the festivities on the fourth of July in the United States. Firecrackers, whistles, sirens, and popping sounds burst across the sky illuminating mountain peaks, harbor boats or quiet villages. Brilliant flashes explode into a myriad of colors, which, as custom has it, will drive out the evil spirit and demons before the New Year. The holy Twelve Nights lasting until Epiphany, January 6, according to legend, contain foreshadowings of the twelve months of the new year. New Year's Eve is the culmination of the period of looking into the future. In contemporary society and in local circles the idea of evil spirits is often unknown, so the fireworks display, festive noisemakers and hoopla are all indications of the gaiety of celebrating and ringing in the new year. Parties and balls are held in restaurants or private clubs as well as in private homes where a more intimate gathering of friends takes place. Throughout the evening there is dancing and a variety of games for adults and young people. 'Bleigiessen' (lead pouring) is done at some parties and provides entertainment for all participants. Lead pellets are melted and dropped into a pan of cold water. The hissing sounds soon disappear as all sorts of figures and shapes form. These are interpreted to be a good luck charm for the next year, although everyone can read what he wants into these shapes. It is said that young girls might discern the face of the man they will marry, others may perceive job potential or possible wealth.

During the evening the 'Feuerzangenbowle' is served at some parties. A sugar cone is placed on a metal tongue suspended over a chafing dish in which red wine is heated. The rum is poured over the sugar cone and lit. The sugar melts and drips into the wine. Each time you pour, you make a wish for the new year. The flame of the cone is kept aglow as long as possible and the higher the flame, the more likely the wish will come true. The beverage at other parties may be 'Glühwein', which contains the same ingredients, but doesn't offer the excitement and anticipation of a 'Feuerzangenbowle'.

At the stroke of midnight church bells ring, guests toast the new year with champagne and make all sorts of noise with party noisemakers. Once the noise has abated somewhat, the hostess may serve a hearty lentil soup. The number of lentils in one's bowl indicates one's prosperity in the new year; the more lentils, the more money in one's pocket! In the Swabian and Franconian areas this soup may also contain 'Spätzle', a noodle.

Another tradition is the serving of herring salad or carp on New Year's Eve. The fish scales on the carp also represent money and are supposed to indicate good luck! Meat salads, rye bread, potato salad, and cold cuts are frequently served. Prior to the drive home some enjoy a cup of black coffee and 'Berliner Pfannkuchen', a doughnut which is especially served at this celebration.

New Year's day finds a more quiet activity at home after the ringing in of the new year. A 'Fleischbraten', (roast) with 'Klösse' (dumplings) are traditional foods to begin the new year in some families. The process of cooking the dumplings by a boiling and expansion symbolizes the wish for the entire year in the sense that there will be a swelling, growth and abundance in all aspects of life.

FEUERZANGENBOWLE
(Fire-Tong or Rum Punch)   Hilde Cox

    1 sugar cone (available at international food shops)
    9½ cups (2liters) Burgundy
    4 cloves
    1 long orange peel or one sliced orange
    1 stick of cinnamon
      juice of one lemon
    2 cups (½liter) rum

Stick cloves into orange peel or orange slice; add with lemon juice and cinnamon stick to the wine which is heating in a chafing dish on the table.
Pour rum into a pitcher, dip sugar into it once, then place it on the 'Feuerzange' on the top of the pot.
Turn off the lights and light the sugar cone.
Each guest takes a turn to pour more rum on the sugar, until it is all melted.

Makes 16-20 servings.

GLÜHWEIN
(Spiced wine)

Hilde Cox

4¼ cups (1 liter) Burgundy
 ¾ cup (150 gr) sugar
 1 stick cinnamon

3 cloves
lemon peel

Heat well; do not boil. Strain into glasses and decorate each one with a strip of lemon peel.

To make a 'Punch' out of a Glühwein, dissolve the sugar first in a cup of hot black tea and add to the wine.
Special 'Glühwein' teabags are also available to give it the characteristic aroma. These teabags can be substituted for the cinnamon, cloves and lemon peel.

Makes 8-10 servings.

HUSAREN PUNSCH
(Elite Artillery Punch)

Elisabeth Kottenhahn

Personal taste should determine the size of bottles used in this recipe which originally comes from Frau Charlotte von Wangenheim, Berlin 1840. Taste as you go and you'll find this punch 'rather splendid'!

2 nice, juicy lemons, grated on 1¾ pounds (800 gr) sugar
½ bottle seltzer water poured over above
1 bottle fine Cognac
2 bottles Bordeaux
4 bottles Rhine wine

1 bottle champagne
½ bottle Port wine

Pour the various beverages over the sugar and seltzer water mixture. It must be served cold. If possible, set on ice. As its name indicates, this is of a rather strong nature.

EIERLIKOR
(Eggnog)

Elli Beck

12 egg yolks
 1 cup (237 ml) brandy (Christian Brothers)
1½ cups (355 ml) heavy cream
 1 cup (130 gr) confectionery sugar
 1 teaspoon vanilla

Mix eggs and sugar in blender. Mix together with brandy and cream.

Serves 6.

PUNSCH FÜR KALTE ABENDE   Heidi Valiente
besonders um die Weihnachtszeit

15 g schwarzer Tee werden mit ½ Liter kochendem Wasser abgebrüht und zugedeckt 15 Minuten stehen gelassen. Dann wird 1 Pfd. an einer Orange abgeriebener Zucker in eine Schüssel gelegt, der Saft von drei Zitronen und zwei Orangen durch eine Serviette an den Zucker geseiht, der geseihte Teeabguss, 1 Liter siedendes Wasser, nach Belieben eine Flasche Rot- oder Weisswein, ¼ - ½ Liter Rum dazugegeben, heiss gestellt, aber ja nicht gekocht und dann in Gläsern serviert.

PUNSCH FÜR KALTE ABENDE
(Punch for cold evenings, especially during the Christmas holidays)

4-5 tea bags (15 gr) black tea
  2 cups (475 ml) boiling water
  2 cups (400 gr) sugar
    juice from 3 lemons
    juice from 2 oranges
  4 cups (950 ml) boiling water
  1 fifth (750 ml) or larger red or white wine
  1 to 2 cups (250-475 ml) rum (according to taste)

Place sugar in large saucepan. Form a well in sugar and place whole orange in center. Spoon sugar over orange entirely. Let stand 1 hour. Heat tea in two cups boiling water. Cover and let stand 15 minutes. Squeeze juice from lemons and oranges. Strain and add to sugar. Add tea (strained if using loose tea), 4 cups boiling water, wine and rum. Heat but do not boil. Serve in glasses.

Makes about 14 8-ounce cups.

KARTOFFELSALAT   Ellen Stixrude
(Potato Salad)

1½ pounds (670 gr) potatoes (6 medium)
  1 medium onion, chopped
  ½ cup (118 ml) beef stock or water
  4 slices (40 gr) bacon sauteed and crumbled
    salt, pepper, vinegar to taste

Wash potatoes and boil in the skin. When cooked, peel the hot potatoes and slice finely (when lukewarm). Add one chopped onion. Sprinkle with ½ cup hot beef stock (or water). Add crumbled bacon, salt, pepper and vinegar to taste. Serve warm.

Serves 6.

HERINGSSALAT

Heli Fink

(Herring Salad)

This is a traditional dish and a 'must' for Christmas or New Year's.

- 14 oz. (400 gr) filets of herring (Matjes)
- 9 oz. (250 gr) cooked lean beef
- 2 apples
- 2 medium onions
- 2-3 large cooked potatoes
- 3 hard boiled eggs
- ½ teaspoon sugar
- 2 medium pickles
- pepper
- vinegar, to taste
- 1 pint (475 ml) sour cream

Chop all ingredients into very small cubes and mix well with the sour cream. If desired, add a few chopped red beets.

Serves 4.

BEEFSTEAK TARTAR

Ralph Gilgenast

(Tartar)

Take a slice of top of round beef finely ground and form into a mound on a serving plate or a board (bread board). Make a small well in the center. Drop a perfect egg yolk carefully into the well and surround the beef with little mounds of black caviar, chopped anchovies, capers, onions (chopped), chives and dill pickles. Add pepper and salt for seasoning. Mix desired amounts with meat and egg and spread on rye or black bread slices. Serve or eat as an open-faced sandwich.

One-half pound beef serves 4.

TARTARBRÖTCHEN

Erika Noll

(Tartar)

Mix raw ground beef (½ lb. serves 4) well with salt, pepper, one egg yolk and finely-diced onion. Then spread thickly on a half of roll or on a slice of rye or black bread. If desired, garnish open-faced sandwich with anchovies and capers.

PIKANTE ZUNGENSCHNITTEN Kris Jeter

(Tasty Sliced Tongue)

This dish was included in my grandmother's 1912 handwritten cookbook.

Cut tongue into slices at an angle; season with salt and pepper and sprinkle with lemon juice; top with a few capers. Roll up slice and secure with thread. Dip rolled tongue into slightly beaten egg; then into breadcrumbs and fry in hot fat until golden brown.

KALTE PLATTE Kris Jeter

(Cold Cut Platter)

Garnished boiled ham and assorted wursts with curly parsley, radishes, hard-boiled eggs and butter.

Cut the ham into strips; arrange in a star pattern and fill out the center with chopped egg yolks. Especially attractive for ham and red wursts is caviar. Add an onion slice to caviar. Decorate grey or light colored wurst with slices of radishes, cut out a hole in the middle and fill with chopped egg. With strips of egg whites make a square and fill it with egg yolks and caviar. Used rolled anchovies, filled with chopped egg whites.
To decorate the platter, cut radishes in half, leaving some greens on the top. Roll butter slices into cones and fill with egg yolks. Decorate with parsley.

FLEISCHSALAT Elisabeth Kottenhahn

(Cooked Meat Salad)

- 12 oz. (300 gr) lean, cooked meat (beef or chicken)
- ¾ cup (125 gr) canned peas
- pickles, diced
- salt, pepper, lemon juice to taste
- mayonnaise to taste

Dice meat finely. Carefully mix with all other ingredients and allow to steep. Let stand in refrigerator. Capers may be added for decoration. Stretch with cooked noodles and add a few drops of vinegar instead of lemon juice. For a Saturday meal, serve with bread, cheese or fresh tomatoes.

WURSTSALAT
Elisabeth Kottenhahn

(Wurst Salad)

14 oz. (400 gr) Jagdwurst
1 onion, finely chopped
  vinegar, oil, salt, pepper, mustard to taste

Dice wurst finely and add to marinade made from other ingredients. Let steep for 2 hours. Serve cold with dark bread and good beer!

KÄSE STIKS
Trudy Gilgenast

(Assorted Cheese Appetizers)

These appetizers are easy to prepare and make a very attractive platter when interspersed with finger sandwiches, sliced or filled eggs and sliced tomatoes. Don't forget parsley!

1. **1 cube of sharp cheese, ½ shelled walnut**

Place nut on top of cheese. Prepare as many as desired.

2. **1 cube of cheese, 1 chunk of pineapple, 1 slice mandarin orange**

Place pineapple and orange on top of cheese and hold together with a toothpick.

3. **1 cube of cheese, 1 slice pimento, 1 olive**

Place pimento and olive on top of cheese and hold together with a toothpick.

SCHINKEN-HAWAII
Walter Gilgenast

(Ham toast-Hawaii style)

2 slices white bread - toasted
2-4 slices boiled ham
2 slices canned pineapple
2 slices mild cheese

Place 1 or 2 slices (according to taste) boiled ham on a slice toasted white bread. Place pineapple slice on top of that and finally a slice of cheese. Broil in oven (or toaster oven) until cheese melts slightly. Serve hot; delicious as a light supper or snack.

Serves 2.

GLÜCKLICHE FLIEGENPILZ - MÄNNER

Lotti Gilgenast

(Good luck mushroom men)

1 slice white bread
1 slice salami
1 hard-boiled egg
  rounded end slice of tomato
  mayonnaise
  black olive

Place salami on bread. Set peeled hard-boiled egg in center of bread in a standing position. Make eyes, nose and mouth with slices of black olive (attach with a toothpick). Top the egg with the rounded end-slice of a tomato and dab with mayonnaise so that it looks like a mushroom! This makes a very attractive platter and can be easily prepared for festive evenings.

RUSSISCHE EIER

Erika Noll

(Russian Eggs)

6 hard-boiled eggs, peeled
3 tablespoons mayonnaise
  salt, pepper to taste

caviar
parsley
2 tomatoes

Cut eggs in half lengthwise or crosswise. Cover with mayonnaise and garnish with caviar, parsley and tomato wedges.

Variation:

Yolks may be removed and mashed. Add salt and pepper, a teaspoon dry mustard and 3 tablespoons mayonnaise. Mix well. Refill egg white and garnish with caviar or anchovies.

ROTE RÜBEN EIER

Marni Stauffer

(Red-Beet Eggs)

1 1-lb. (454 gr) can beets
1 cup (237 ml) vinegar
¾ cup (150 gr) sugar
1 tablespoon salt

1 tablespoon mixed pickling spices
6 hard-boiled eggs, peeled
1 medium onion, thinly sliced
  and separated into rings

Drain beets, reserving liquid. Pour liquid into a glass jar or bowl. Add vinegar, sugar, salt and spices, stirring until sugar dissolves. Add beets, eggs and onion. Chill at least 2 hours before serving. Serve drained eggs in one dish, beets and onions in another.

GURKENSCHIFFCHEN
(Cucumber boats)

Kris Jeter

These two recipes were included in my grandmother's handwritten 1912 German cookbook.

Put some clear aspic onto a platter to simulate water. Cut two large or three small pickled cucumbers in half; scrape out soft parts. Insert a long spaghetti firmly into the middle as a mast; use a piece of an onion as a sail. Fill the insides of the cucumbers with all kinds of garnishes: **pickled mushrooms, capers, red beets, mixed pickles, pearl onions, asparagus tips, cauliflowers, hard boiled eggs, etc.**
Keep the colors harmonious; use green on red, yellow on brown, accentuate with white.
As rudders use teaspoons; cover the edge of the platter with parsley leaves to mark the shore. The boats can also be filled with Italian salad or meat salad. They make a nice breakfast for men or evening surprise at a party.

SAURE LINSEN MIT SPÄTZLE
(Sour Lentils with noodles)

Pauline Zistl

This is one of my favorites.

Sour Lentil Soup:
1½ cups (360 ml or 340 gr) lentils
  1 medium onion, diced
  2 quarts (1 and 9/10 liters) water
4-5 tablespoons margarine
2-3 tablespoons flour
1-2 beef bouillon cubes
  2 tablespoons vinegar, or to taste

Cook the lentils with diced onion in water for about ½ hour or until soft. In a skillet melt the margarine, add flour and use a wooden spoon to stir steadily until the flour becomes dark brown. Add the browned flour, bouillon cubes and vinegar to the cooked lentils and simmer 15-20 minutes.

Spätzle:
  2 cups (230 gr) flour
  4 eggs
1-2 tablespoons lukewarm water
   salt to taste

Mix and beat all ingredients together until the dough is very smooth and soft with bubbles; about 5 minutes of steady beating. I now have a Spätzle machine but for many years I made these noodles by hand, placing a batch of dough on a special small board and scraping small slivers of the dough with a knife into the boiling water. The noodles should cook about 3-4 minutes.

Serves 8-10.

LINSENSUPPE

Alma M. DeMott

(Lentil Soup)

Mother always made this for our lunch on cold, windy or rainy days. I can remember how good it smelled and tasted when I came home from school for lunch. Somehow it doesn't taste as good now as it did then; mother had a special knack.

1 1-pound (454 gr) package of lentils covered with water; bring to a full boil. Strain, cover again with boiling water. Add an onion studded with six cloves, a couple of bay leaves, salt and pepper.
Let simmer about two hours, then add some bacon that has been fried until crisp and cut up. We always put in a few frankfurters as well.

Serves 6.

ROSTBRATEN

Regina Ross

(Steak)

Any top grade steak, such as New York strip, T-bone or tenderloin, ⅝ inch thick, is suitable. If too thick, pound to proper size.

1 steak per person
5 very thin slices of a medium onion per steak
1 teaspoon butter for one pan
1 tablespoon water per steak
  salt and pepper
  heavy frying pan

Trim all fat and bone from meat. Salt and pepper on both sides. Heat frying pan over high heat, melt butter (it should get brown right away), add steak and onion. When first side is browned (this takes only 2-3 minutes), turn meat over and lower heat to medium. Stir onions frequently, so they won't burn. The overall cooking time for the steak is 5-6 minutes. It will be barely pink inside.

Remove steak to a warm plate. Add water to the pan and scrape the juices and onions together. Pour over the meat and serve with parsley potatoes (boiled potatoes tossed with hot melted butter and chopped fresh parsley).

BAYRISCHE KNÖDEL

Lisa Weinauer

(Potato Dumplings)

4-5 potatoes (boiled)
8-10 potatoes (raw)
2-3 eggs
    bread croutons
    pinch of salt

Note: U.S. #1 potatoes are best to use because of their starch content.

Boil 4-5 potatoes with their jackets on. Cool, peel and grate or mash finely.

Peel about twice as many raw potatoes and grate. Put into towel and squeeze out as much liquid as possible, twisting top tightly. Do not expose to air, as potatoes will darken.

In large bowl combine the two potato preparations, add 2-3 eggs, according to the volume, a pinch of salt. Form a test dumpling with wet hands. Put a few pieces of bread croutons into center and form complete dumpling the size of a lemon or small apple.

Drop into boiling salted water. If dumpling does not hold together, add flour to the mixture.

When all dumplings come to the surface of boiling water, let them boil about 3 or 4 minutes. Take one out with a slotted spoon and cut in half. Center should be dry, not soggy.

These are great with roast goose or pork roast, both of which have a rich gravy.

Any leftovers, sliced and fried will be liked as well as the first dumplings. So, make a few extra for a leftover supper.

SEIDENKLÖSSE

Elli Beck

(Dumplings)

3 lbs. potatoes
2 eggs
8 oz. (227 gr) potato starch (available at international food shops)

Boil potatoes, then put through ricer; add salt and remaining ingredients and mix well. Form dumplings and drop into boiling water and simmer about 20 minutes.

GRÜNE KLÖSSE

Kurt Runge

(Raw potato dumplings)

Use ten medium to large potatoes. Don't use new potatoes. Boil and peel five of them. When done, press through ricer or mash and set aside. Grate the 5 raw potatoes, squeeze dry in a tea towel (a little at a time). Set the resulting liquid aside.

Combine riced and grated raw potatoes in a bowl. Add a little salt, one beaten egg, one cup of croutons and two tablespoons of cream of wheat (the egg and cream of wheat act as binders).

Cover mixture and set aside about one hour. Pour off raw potato liquid and add back any settled out starch to mixture. Form in 2" diameter dumplings. Cook for about 15 minutes in simmering water. If water boils too vigorously, dumplings will disentegrate. This stage is critical; success frequently depends on type of potatoes. If dumplings fall apart too much, add more cream of wheat. After boiling about 10 minutes, dumplings should rise to surface. Serve with Sauerbraten!

MUTTIS BERLINER PFANNEKUCHEN

Trudy Rueggeberg

(Mother's Berliner donuts)

All ingredients, including eggs, must be warm (room temperature)

    1 small square compressed yeast (or equivalent in weight, dried)
    ⅓ cup (80 ml) warm water
    4 cups (460 gr) all purpose flour
    ¼ lb. (115 gr) butter (or half butter, half margarine)
    ½ cup (100 gr) granulated sugar
    1 teaspoon salt
    2 eggs
    grated rind of 1 lemon
    1 cup (237 ml) milk
    1 12 oz. jar Damson plum jam
      Crisco for deep frying

Crumble yeast in bowl, add warm water. When dissolved, add about 1 cup (115 gr) of the flour. Beat. Cover. Let rise approximately 15 minutes.

In the meantime cream the butter (not too soft before creaming), with the sugar, then add the salt, add the eggs, one at a time, beat with Mixmaster for 6-8 minutes. Add lemon rind.

After yeast dough has risen, add it to butter, sugar, and egg mixture. Gradually add flour - 1 cup (150 gr) at a time alternating with milk. Beat by hand for about 8 to 10 minutes.

Set cake mixture into two large bowls, sprinkle top with flour, cover with tea towel - let rise for 2 or 3 hours in a warm place, until batter has doubled in bulk and is very light.

Then knead dough very well. Roll out small portions of batter on floured board until about ⅜" thick. Figuring with rectangles approx. 2½ x 5", place about 1 level tsp. of preserves in center of one half of rectangle, fold other half over same. Then use donut cutter or wine glass to cut circular shape, as close to 2½ inches as possible. Pinch edges of donut together firmly with fingers, so that filling can't escape.

Place Berliner on lightly floured board, cover with towel, let rise. After 20 minutes, turn over on other side and let rise 10-15 additional minutes, also covered.

When they feel light, drop into Crisco in deep fryer (400 - 425°) 3 to 4 at a time. Let fry 2-3 minutes on each side. Place into drip basket, then on brown paper to absorb fat. Roll donuts in mixture of sugar and cinnamon, to taste.

Makes 20 donuts.

GÖTTERSPEISE

Ina Hartmann

(A dish pleasing to the Gods)

This dish is my own creation and is served as a special treat for parties or for my Kaffeeklatsch. It has been very popular in our family in Germany and also here in the U.S. I make it also for special family gatherings and for New Year's Eve.

2 packages (12 each) Ladyfingers
1 cup (237 ml) milk
2-3 tablespoons rum

Creme:
3 large (4 small) egg yolks
¼ lb. (114 gr) margarine
1 cup (200 gr) sugar
1 teaspoon vanilla
whipped cream or Coolwhip

Soak ladyfingers (broken up into pieces) in milk and rum. When well soaked, put into desired form (glass dish or serving container). Make creme mixture by combining egg yolks, margarine, sugar, and vanilla and mix well to a foamy-like substance. Pour over the ladyfinger mixture and cool in refrigerator at least one hour.

Before serving, garnish with whipped cream (or Coolwhip) and fruits, pralines or almonds.

FASCHING
(Carnival and Lent)

February is the time of carnival - those weeks prior to Ash Wednesday, celebrated throughout West Germany but especially in Cologne, along the Rhine, in Mainz and in Munich. This period of sensuous freedom and boundless celebration is known as Fastnacht in southern Germany, as Fasching in Munich, and Fastelovend in the Rhineland. Although it officially begins on November 11 at 11:11 p.m., the frantic fanfare of activity is delayed until after Christmas and Epiphany.

Religious, hedonistic and superstitious roots all contribute to the numerous customs practiced in modern times. Since this is the season bordering between winter and spring, man is thought to be in conflict with winter and demonic spirits. By wearing masks and costumes he gains strength in driving out these forces and in triumphing over them. Religious origins indicate that man desires a period of 'eat, drink and be merry' prior to the forty days of lenten abstinence. Again the masquerade permits him to pose as a fool and free himself from all daily concerns and inhibitions.

The first official recognition of Fasching came from the City Council of Munich in 1537, but the festivities go back at least two more centuries. It is first mentioned in German writings dating back to 1359. The early celebrations featured sleigh rides and tournaments in which knights jousted wearing small wooden barrels on their heads instead of helmets. The first 'fast nacht' dances were held in a special hall built by the council.

Traditions continued to be added and in 1894 the well-organized balls began. (In Munich today there are more than 3,000 costume balls during the festival!) It was at this time that the first prince was crowned, the first big parade initiated and decorated floats bounced through the decorated streets. In 1908 an organization was founded to maintain the artistic standards of the event.

Fertility rites played an important role and peas, nuts, rice and eggs served as manifestations of virility. Current customs in the throwing of confetti also symbolize fertility. This paper snow-like effect is cheaper and easier to use. (The American custom of throwing confetti and rice at weddings indicates a wish for happiness and a fruitful union).

Fasching is unquestionably a time of parades, costumes, drinking, dancing and celebrating in which everyone lets it 'all hang out'. All sorts of costume balls take place - students, butchers, bakers, brewers to mention only a few. These are masquerade affairs and often one never knows with whom one dances or spends the evening! Traditionally, a Fasching 'König' (king) and 'Königin' (queen) are crowned and they rule for the season by attending balls, parties and numerous official functions of the region. These events today have more political overtones and politicians enjoy the opportunity of poking fun at one another, for it is only during the carnival season that they can get away with it. Everyone is in a jovial mood; 'Gemütlichkeit' reigns and one's actions are not taken seriously.

Germans in the Wilmington area celebrate in clubs as well as in private homes. Although these masquerade parties are primarily for adults, some families permit their children and those of friends to share in the costume merrymaking. Games in which everyone participates provide the entertainment until it is time to unmask and identify oneself. Prizes are awarded to the funniest, most original and most beautiful costumes. Some local churches also sponsor a program on Fastnacht designed to entertain, poke fun and permit participants to make a spectacle of themselves through songs, dances and skits. A traditional refreshment served on Shrove Tuesday is the Fastnacht 'Krapfen', the doughnuts.

Food is, of course, an important part of the feasting before the forty days of fasting between Ash Wednesday and Easter. Whether the celebration takes place in a public hall or restaurant or in a private home, one can be assured of a 'fools paradise' with mountains of food and liters of alcohol.

On 'Rosenmontag' everyone who is not wearing a costume must buy his friend a rose as punishment. This day climaxes all merrymaking with parades, parties and dancing in the streets. Shrove Tuesday winds down the celebrating with a last get-together for the 'Kehraus', when literally everything and everyone is 'swept out with a broom' into the streets at the stroke of midnight. Ash Wednesday has begun. A period of sobriety and contemplation commences. Numerous food customs reflect the abstinence of meat on certain holy days and the tendency to eat a simpler fare during the lenten days.

FASTNACHTS
(Doughnuts)

Sue Schley

Every Shrove Tuesday the family gathers and makes the Fastnachts together. This recipe has been used by my family since the 1730's when they came over from Bavaria.

    1 cup (237 ml or 250 gr) hot sieved potatoes
    1 cup (200 gr) sugar
    1 cup (237 ml) scalding milk
    ½ cup (118 ml) lukewarm water (110° F.)
       about 5½ cups (630 gr) flour
    1 cup (227 gr) shortening
    1 teaspoon salt
    2 packages yeast
    2 beaten eggs or 3 egg whites

Combine potatoes, shortening, sugar and salt; stir until smooth. Add hot milk and allow to cool until lukewarm. Dissolve yeast in lukewarm water and milk mixture with beaten eggs. Add half of the flour and beat vigorously until satin smooth. Continue adding flour until a stiff batter is formed. Turn onto floured surface and knead lightly. Place in greased bowl, cover and let rise until light (double in size). Roll out on floured board, cut and fry in deep fat. Shake in confectioner's sugar or glaze as desired.

BERLINER KRAPFEN oder
FASCHINGSKRAPFEN
(Jelly Doughnuts)

Helga Herglotz-Kissell

    3-4 cups (350-460 gr) unsifted flour
     ¼   cup (50 gr) sugar
    1½   teaspoon salt
    1¼   cup (320 ml) warm water (105-115°)
     1   package active dry yeast
     2   egg yolks, beaten
     ¼   cup (57 gr) butter or margarine
         grated rind of one lemon
     ¼   cup (60 ml) plum or apricot jam

Mix 2 cups (230 gr) flour with sugar and salt. Make a well in the center and add ¼ (60 ml) cup warm water and the yeast. Allow to rise 20 minutes. Add egg yolks, remaining water, and butter. Beat until well blended. Add lemon rind and remaining flour until a soft dough is formed. Knead 5-10 minutes until dough is smooth and elastic. Place dough in a lightly greased bowl.

Cover and let rise in a warm place until doubled in bulk, about 1½ hours. Punch dough down. On lightly floured board roll dough ¼ inch thick. Cut dough into 2-inch (5 cm) rounds. On half of the rounds place about 1 teaspoon of jam or jelly. Moisten edges with water. Place a second round on top. Press firmly to seal edges. Let rise 15 minutes. Fry in deep fat heated to 375° for 4 minutes on each side or until browned. Cut into first doughnut to be sure it is done in the center. Drain on absorbent paper and sprinkle with lots of sugar as the doughnuts are not sweet.

Makes 24 doughnuts.

KRAPFEN
(Raisin Doughnuts)

Anna Herold

- 2 packages dry yeast
- 1 cup (237 ml) milk
- 1 cup (237 ml) cream
- ½ teaspoon salt
- ½ cup (100 gr) sugar
- 6 eggs beaten
- 1 cup (170 gr) raisins
- 4 cups (460 gr) flour

Dissolve yeast in 2 tablespoons (30 ml) warm water. Combine milk and cream (at room temperature), salt and sugar. Add yeast and mix well. Blend in eggs, mix thoroughly. Add raisins and flour to make a soft dough. Let rise 2-3 hours.
Drop from tablespoon into hot lard or oil. Fry until brown.
Roll in sugar and a little cinnamon.

Yields 5-6 doz.

EIERKUCHEN
(Pancakes)

Elsie Roser Lister

My mother often baked these pancakes, but especially on Fastnacht, the day before Ash Wednesday. We called it 'pancake day' at home.

- 2 cups (230 gr) flour
- 2-3 eggs
- 1 teaspoon sugar
- 1 teaspoon salt
- 2 cups (475 ml) milk

Mix all ingredients together and fry in a frying pan. Make thin pancakes, the size of the pan. Fry golden brown on both sides and serve with fruit such as peaches, sausage and German potato salad.

SCHEITERHAUFEN

Heidi Valiente

eine Lentenkost - Schwäbisch

6 Semmeln werden in Scheiben geschnitten, in gesüsste kalte Milch eingetaucht und lagenweise abwechselnd mit gut gereinigten Weinbeeren und fein geschnittenen, mit Zucker und Zimt bestreuten Äpfeln in eine mit Butter bestrichene Form gegeben. Die Decklage soll von Semmelscheiben sein. Dann werden 4 Eier mit ½ Liter Milch verklopft, Zucker und Zimt nach Geschmack beigegeben und über die Scheiben gegossen. Obenauf legt man noch einige Stückchen Butter und bäckt die Masse ½ Stunde im Rohr bei 350° F.

SCHEITERHAUFEN
(Swabian Lenten Dish)

6 Kaiser rolls	2 cups (475 ml) milk
sugar	4 eggs
cinnamon	apple slices, raisins

Cut rolls into slices, soak in 1 cup (237 ml) cold milk somewhat sweetened to taste and place 1 layer in a greased baking pan. Alternate layers of seedless white raisins and apple slices sprinkled with a sugar and cinnamon mixture. The top layer should consist only of the roll mixture. Set aside. Beat 4 eggs in 1 cup (237 ml) milk, add sugar and cinnamon to taste. Pour this mixture over the roll mixture. Dot with several pats of butter and bake 30 minutes at 350° F.

KAISERSCHMARREN

Leni Holzhauser

(Emperor's Pancakes)

4 eggs (separated)	1 cup (237 ml) milk
5 tablespoons sugar	4 tablespoons butter
1 cup (115 gr) flour	3 tablespoons raisins

In a bowl mix 4 egg yolks with 3 tablespoons sugar, gradually beat in 1 cup of flour and milk and beat the mixture until it is smooth. In another bowl beat 4 egg whites with a pinch of salt until they are stiff but not dry. Add one-fourth of the whites to the yolk mixture and fold them gently but thoroughly. Pour the yolk mixture over the remaining whites and fold them in thoroughly. Heat 2 tablespoons butter in a heavy 12-inch skillet and pour in the batter. Cook the pancake over moderate heat until it is brown, turn it and brown the other side (it does not matter if the pancake tears while turning).

Sprinkle the pancake with 3 tablespoons raisins. Tear the pancake into large pieces with 2 forks, add 2 tablespoons butter and sprinkle the pieces with 1 to 2 tablespoons sugar. Stir the pieces gently and shake the pan for a few minutes until they are lightly glazed. Sprinkle the Kaiserschmarren with sifted confectioner's sugar and serve it with rum-laced stewed plums or raspberry syrup.

Serves 4-6

KIRSCHENJOKEL
(Cherry Souffle)

Anke Becker

An ideal dish for a meatless meal!

    6 rolls
    1 stick (½ cup or 125 gr) butter
    ¾ cup plus 2 tablespoons (200 gr) sugar
    4 eggs, separated
    1 teaspoon ground cinnamon
    2 oz (60 gr) almonds
    2¼ cups (½ liter) milk
    2¼ pounds (1000 gr) canned, pitted cherries, drained
       rind of ½ lemon, grated

Cut rolls into slices, moisten with milk. Let stand for some time. Stir butter, add sugar and egg yolks. Mix with rolls. Let stand for ½ hour. Blend thoroughly with the stiffly beaten egg whites, spices and cherries. Spread in greased casserole or baking dish. Bake at 350° F. for 1 hour.

EIERNOCKERL
(Egg Dumpling)

Eugenia Slavov

1¾ cups (200 gr) flour
1½ tablespoons shortening
1¼ cups (3/10 liter) milk
Sauce:
1-2 eggs

salt, to taste
salted boiling water
1 tablespoon butter

2 tablespoons cream

Beat shortening to a fluffy consistency. Add egg, flour, milk and salt and beat until mixture forms a soft dough which does not cling to wooden spoon. Form the dough into small dumpling or crescent shapes, drop into salted boiling water and cook for 10 minutes. Then remove with a slotted spoon or sieve, rinse with cold water and put into hot butter. Pour a sauce made of beaten eggs and cream over the dumplings and let simmer until the eggs thicken.

MAULTASCHEN

Abby Hartmann

(Mouth Pockets or Filled Noodles)

This is about as Swabian a dish as you can get. Traditionally this has always been very popular in our family (Rottweil/Neckar) for generations. A non-meat dish, it was frequently cooked during the Lenten season. You do not find it anywhere north of Stuttgart and an uncle who now lives in Koblenz stocks up on a commercial source of Maultaschen in Stuttgart-Cannstatt on return trips from southern Europe.

We cook Maultaschen as a special traditional treat and as a surprise for our Swabian relatives and friends. Although it is time consuming to prepare, it can be "stretched" to cover several meals in variations, each one unique and tasty in its own right. Serve it as a soup with bouillon broth (Suppenswaben), sliced and fried with eggs or plain. Kopfsalat (lettuce salad) goes very well with it. Maultaschen are also good when cold and in our home they never last long because of frequent refrigerator "raids". This continuing tradition of raiding presents a problem and serves as well as a compliment to the cook.

Dough:
- 4-5 eggs
- 4 tablespoons water (or milk)
- 4 cups (460 gr) flour
- 1 teaspoon salt

Filling:
- 1 lb. (454 gr) spinach (cooked, chopped and drained)
- 1 onion (finely diced)
- parsley (chopped)
- 4-6 eggs
- 8 slices bread
- ½ cup (118 ml) water
- salt and pepper

Beat eggs with water, add salt. Sift half of flour onto a floured board (or in a bowl) and make a well. Pour beaten egg mixture into well and gradually work in flour until dough holds together. Add remainder of flour and knead dough for 5+ minutes until smooth and elastic. Let stand for 10 minutes so that it will dry out. Then roll out dough into thin sections. Cut dough into 3 in. squares. Put a teaspoonful of filling in center of each square and fold in half to form Taschen - pockets. Press edges together firmly and crimp edges with a fork. Drop into boiling water and cook for 15 minutes. Drain and serve as desired (in a soup or with melted butter, etc.).

To make filling, mix cooked drained spinach and onion together. Soak bread slices in water, squeeze dry and crumble bread into spinach mixture. Mix in eggs, parsley, salt and pepper and mix thoroughly. Fill into dough mixture which has been rolled out and cut as described above.

PFLAUMENKNÖDEL AUS TOPFENTEIG

Elnora (Toots) Schweiger

(Cottage Cheese Plum Dumplings)

Force through a food mill or sieve into a bowl ½ lb. (227 gr) firmly packed dry cottage cheese.
Sift together and set aside
   1 cup (115 gr) flour
   ¼ teaspoon salt

Prepare 3 cups (about 3 slices) soft bread crumbs. Cream until soft 2 tablespoons butter; add 2 eggs well beaten. Beat together well. Blend in cottage cheese and bread crumbs. Add flour and beat thoroughly. Chill in refrigerator 1 hour. Meanwhile rinse and cut almost into halves and remove pits from 4 blue plums.
Set out 4 cubes of sugar. Insert one cube into each plum. When dough is chilled, divide into four portions, shape one portion of dough around each plum being sure to completely cover plum.
Seal well.
Heat to boiling in large heavy saucepan 2 qts. (2 liters) water. Carefully drop dumplings into boiling water. Cook for 10 minutes or until dumplings come to surface. Remove carefully with slotted spoon and serve with vanilla sauce.

Vanilla Sauce

Sift together in top of double boiler
   1 cup (200 gr) sugar
   2 tablespoons cornstarch
   ¼ teaspoon salt

Add and stir well 2 cups (474 ml) boiling water. Stir until mixture comes to a boil and cook for 3 minutes. Place over simmering water. Cover and cook 12 minutes stirring a few times. Vigorously stir about 3 tablespoons of hot mixture into 1 egg yolk, slightly beaten. Blend this into mixture in double boiler. Cook slowly for 3-5 minutes; stir to keep mixture cooking evenly. Remove from heat and blend in

   ¼ cup (57 gr) butter
   2 teaspoons vanilla
   ¼ teaspoon nutmeg

Mixture is now ready to serve with dumplings.

Makes 4.

DAMPFNUDELN

½ kg Mehl
1 Teel. Salz
60-80 g Zucker
80 g Butter

1 Ei
¼ l Milch
20 g Hefe

Zum Aufziehen in einer Pfanne mit Deckel etwa 28 cm Durchmesser:
2 mal je ⅛ l Wasser
1 Teel. Salz
1 Essl. Fett

Mit den angegebenen Zutaten bereitet man einen glatten Hefeteig, den man in die Wärme stellt. Ist er gegangen, sticht man mit einem Esslöffel runde Küchlein ab, nicht so klein. Diese setzt man auf ein mit Mehl bestäubtes Brett und lässt sie, mit einem Tuch bedeckt, gehen.

In einer eisernen Pfanne lässt man Fett zergehen, gibt Salz dazu, setzt die Küchlein hinein, nicht zu eng, damit sie aufgehen können, gibt ⅛ l Wasser kalt hinzu, deckt den Topf mit einem gut schliessenden Deckel zu und lässt die Dampfnudeln auf schwach mässiger Hitze 15-20 Minuten langsam aufziehen. Sobald in der Pfanne ein krachendes Geräusch zu hören ist, wird der Deckel sehr vorsichtig abgenommen, so dass keine Wassertropfen auf das Gebäck fallen. Der Boden muss eine schön goldgelbe Farbe haben. Die Dampfnudeln werden mit einem Schaufelchen herausgenommen, auf eine Platte gesetzt, mit Vanillesosse gereicht.

DAMPFNUDELN
(Steamed Sweet Dumplings)

4¼ cups (½ kilogram) flour
1 teaspoon salt
⅓ cup (60-80 gr) sugar
¼ cup (80 gr) butter
1 egg
1 cup plus 2 tablespoons (¼ liter) milk
1 pkg dry yeast, (20 gr)

Prepare smooth yeast dough with the above ingredients. Place in a draft-free warm place. When the dough has risen, form small cakes or balls with a tablespoon. Don't form them too small. Place these on a lightly floured board and cover them with a towel and let rise again.

In a 9-inch (28 cm) skillet which has tight-fitting lid, melt 1 tablespoon fat and add 1 teaspoon salt. Place about half the balls in the pan so they are not crowded, allowing room for expansion. Add ½ cup (⅛ liter) <u>cold</u> water and cover. Simmer for 15-20 minutes as they rise. As soon as a sizzling sound is heard, remove the lid carefully so that not a drop of water falls onto the

dumplings. The bottom must have a nice gold-yellow color. Remove with a spatula and serve with vanilla sauce.
Repeat procedure with the fat, salt and water to steam remaining dumplings.

DAMPFNUDELN
Anita Malanowicz
(Steamed Sweet Dumplings)

Once your family has tried them, they'll want them again!
You'll need:
a large frying pan with a fitted lid (teflon or ironstone)
a large mixing bowl (not metal, it's too cold)
It's best to have bowl and ingredients at least at room temperature if not warmer.

2 packages dry yeast ⎫
2 teaspoons sugar ⎭ mix with a little of the milk to dissolve
2 lbs. or 8 cups (920 gr) flour plus 1 cup (115 gr) for later
4 teaspoons salt   1½ cups (355 ml) milk
¼ lb. (57 gr) butter   1 cup (237 ml) water
½ cup (110 gr) sugar   1 cup (237 ml) veg. oil or shortening

Mix in large bowl: 8 cups flour, ½ cup sugar, 1 teaspoon salt. In center of this make a hole, the size of a fist, pour yeast mixture, mix with a little flour and let rise for 20 minutes. Now add the ¼ lb. of very soft butter and start mixing by hand. Keep adding a little milk and water until all flour, milk and water has been kneaded in. By now, dough should be coming off the bowl. Let rise for 30 minutes.
Make a solution of 3 cups water and 3 teaspoons salt. Set aside.
(Sprinkle flour on 2 large cutting boards or a surface that can be kept warm for dough to rise a third time).
After dough in bowl has risen, dip hand in flour and dust dough with a little flour to keep it from sticking to hand and knead it together again. Work it a little while longer - dusting with flour till it comes off bowl each time.
Now form balls, about the size of tennis balls, and set on floured board. Let rise about 1 hour (make thumbprint in center, when gone, they're ready to bake).

In frying pan put ½ cup oil, ¾ cup water and one teaspoon salt. Bring to boil. Set 4 dumplings carefully into this, cover and fry at low medium heat for 15 minutes and at medium heat for 10 more minutes. Turn pan to fry even. **All** water **must** boil away and the dumplings must fry in oil. (Hint: when steam no longer smells like dough, but smells baked, they should be ready). Lift lid VERY QUICKLY off pan so that drops will not fall on dumplings. With spatula lift dumplings onto platter. Repeat frying until all dumplings have been baked. Tops should be white, bottoms fried brown.
Serve warm with a good soup or a vanilla sauce for a meatless supper. Delicious!

Yields about 10 or 12.

DAMPFNUDELN
Lia Wycoff

(Steamed Sweet Dumplings)

My grandmother was a great cook and she saw to it that her children and grandchildren became skilled as well. It is a little work to prepare these dishes, but well worth the effort. My family loves eating the Dampfnudeln, especially on a cold winter's evening.

Set out a heavy 10 inch skillet with a tight-fitting lid.

Scald ½ cup (118 ml) milk
Meanwhile, soften
  ½ package (1 teaspoon) active dry yeast in
  2 tablespoons warm water, 110°F - 115°F
Let stand 5 - 10 minutes.
In a large bowl put
  ¼ cup (57 gr) butter
  ⅓ cup (75 gr) sugar
  ¼ teaspoon salt
Immediately pour scalded milk over ingredients in bowl. When lukewarm, blend in, beating until smooth
  1 cup (115 gr) sifted flour
Stir softened yeast and add, mixing well.
Measure
  2 - 2½ cups (300-375 gr) sifted flour
Add about one half of the flour to yeast mixture and beat until very smooth. Beat in.
  2 eggs, well beaten.
Add enough of remaining flour to make a soft dough. Turn dough onto lightly floured surface and let rest 5 to 10 minutes. Now knead dough for 8 - 10 minutes. Form dough into ball and place in a greased deep bowl. Turn dough to bring greased surface to top. Cover with waxed paper and a towel and let stand in a warm, draft-free place (about 80°F) until dough has doubled in size. Punch dough down and turn out on lightly floured board. Shape dough into balls about 1 ½ inches in diameter. Cover again with waxed paper and towel and let rise on board until balls are doubled.
Put into the skillet

1½ cups (355 ml) milk
  1 tablespoon butter
  1 tablespoon sugar

Place about 7 of the balls into the skillet. Do not set them too close together. Cover and cook over high heat until steam appears. Reduce heat and cook 30 minutes or until steaming stops. Do **not** remove cover during cooking!
Carefully remove dumplings with a slotted spoon to serving dishes and serve with a wine sauce.

KARTOFFELPUFFER

Elly Gilgenast

(Potato Pancakes)

2 lbs. (about 6 medium/large)potatoes, peeled and quartered (prepare potatoes immediately before serving as potatoes turn dark when grated.)
1 large onion, quartered
½ cup (118 ml) milk
½ to 1 cup (58-115 gr) flour (use ½ cup flour with drier potatoes; up to 1 cup with more watery potatoes
2 teaspoons salt
2 eggs

Grate potatoes and onion into a bowl. Add milk, then stir in flour, salt, eggs, and mix well. In large heavy skillet heat ½ inch frying oil until hot. Drop potato batter (¼ cup per pancake) into skillet and fry until golden brown and crisp on both sides. Drain on paper towel. Serve with fruit compote or jelly.

Serves 6.

KARTOFFELPUFFER

Anna Herold

(Potato Pancakes)

6 large potatoes, grated
1 large onion, grated
2 - 3 eggs, well beaten
½ teaspoon sugar
2 tablespoons flour
2 tablespoons fine bread crumbs
1 teaspoon salt, a little pepper

Grate the potatoes in a deep bowl of water blended with lemon juice. This keeps the potatoes white (otherwise they turn dark as soon as grated). When potatoes are grated, press out the water. Add the rest of the ingredients and mix well.
(For a little change, grate 1 large carrot with the potatoes). Have a large frying pan very hot with oil or shortening, drop by spoonful and fry until brown on both sides.

Serves 6 - 8

BAYERISCHE BROTKNÖDEL

(Bavarian Bread Dumplings)

Pauline Zistl

1 1-lb. (454 gr) loaf of white bread (or equivalent rolls)
¾ cup (178 ml) milk   1 medium onion
3 eggs   2 - 3 tablespoons flour

This is one of my husband's favorites.
We prefer to use rolls for these dumplings but white bread will also do. The rolls or bread should be about 4 days old, stale enough to absorb the liquid in the recipe.
Dice the bread in ½" cubes. Dice and lightly brown the onions in a pan with some margarine. In a large mixing bowl combine the bread cubes, onion and eggs. Add milk, a little at a time, to moisten but not soak bread. Add flour, a little at a time, to bind the mixture well together. Form into balls, about the size of a small fist and place in boiling water (ice cream scoop can be used to make the balls and drop them into boiling water). The dumplings must cook for 10 - 15 minutes until inside of the dumpling is well done. These knöedel can be served with goulash or any other meat having gravy. They are also good several days later, fried in slices much like potatoes.

BROTKNÖDEL

(Bread Dumplings)

Elli Beck

1 loaf white bread   4 eggs
2 cups (474 ml) boiling milk   salt and pepper
3 - 4 tablespoons flour

Break up bread into small pieces, pour boiling milk over and cover. Let stand about 1 hour. Then mix in remaining ingredients. Form dumplings, drop into boiling salt water and simmer 25 - 30 minutes.

GRIESSNOCKERLSUPPE

(Farina or Cream of Wheat Soup)

Magda Ruoff

3 tablespoons (40 gr) butter   pinch of salt
1 egg   6½ cups (1½ liters) chicken stock
5 tablespoons (60 gr) farina or cream of wheat

Cream butter, add egg and some farina. Beat until smooth. Add remainder of farina and salt and mix thoroughly. Let batter stand for 15 minutes. Form small dumplings (Nockerl) with two teaspoons. Dip teaspoons into cold water after forming each dumpling. Drop dumplings into boiling broth and let simmer for 20 - 25 minutes.

FLÄDLESUPPE

Ingrid Torres

(Soup with pancake strips)

A popular soup from southern Germany!

1 egg	1 teaspoon chopped parsley
dash of salt	or small bunch fresh chives)
½ cup (58 gr) all purpose flour	2 tablespoons butter
½ cup (118 ml) water	4½ cups (1 liter) clear beef broth

Put flour into a bowl. Make a well in the middle and add salt and egg. Starting from the middle, stir and mix egg and flour, gradually adding water. Mix thoroughly after each addition to make a thin batter. Finally add chopped parsley (or chives).

Bake very thin pancakes, turning each pancake once until it is a deep golden color on both sides.

Cut the pancakes into very thin strips. Heat the broth, add the pancake strips and serve at once.

Serves 4.

PFANNKUCHENSUPPE

Magda Ruoff

(Pancake Soup)

Just use a basic "crepes" recipe and make the pancake nice and thin. Roll the crepe and cut ¼ inch strips. Put these into soup bowl or tureen and pour boiling stock over them. Add finely cut chives as a final garnish.

OSTERN
(Easter)

Although all seasons play an important part in the lives of the Germans, the awakening of nature after the sterility of winter, the water released from the ice, the traditions of the Easter rabbit and Easter eggs all bring a special joy of renewal and hope in the spring. Easter and spring customs have evolved often simultaneously over the years and numerous Christian customs are reflected in this season. In pre-Christian days Easter was observed as a heathen spring festival. The name itself 'Ostern' (Easter) points to a sun cult. This may indicate a festival in honor of the spring goddess 'Ostara' or it may refer to the spring sun rising with increasing warmth in the 'Osten' (east). The goddess Ostara was known to the Anglo-Saxons as Eastre or Eoster. The German Easter Festival, celebrated as a reawakening of nature, is clearly so indicated in the name, so it was natural for the Christian church to take over this festival and its customs and apply them to the worship of the risen Christ. Easter, the Resurrection of Jesus Christ on the third day after the crucifixion, is the oldest Christian feast introduced in the second century. Palm Sunday, 'Gründonnerstag' (Green or Maundy Thursday) and 'Karfreitag' (Good Friday) are important and sacred holy days preceding Easter; holy week climaxes the quiet time of the lenten season. Good Friday is still observed by many for its religious significance and it is a time to reflect. Easter Sunday is celebrated as the apex of holy days; in Catholic churches first communions are also celebrated.

One of the most popular secular traditions during the week prior to Easter is the coloring and hand decorating of Easter eggs. Children and adults enjoy creating original designs on hard-cooked eggs or on the more delicate shell of the blown-out egg. Some traditions passed down in families incorporate batik style or scratching designs. Some use a technique which scratches a pattern with acid or lemon juice, others use a melted candle wax on the shell and dye the egg in different colors. The dyes used are commercial or made out of crepe paper. These eggs are often given as a gift to friends or used to decorate an Easter egg tree. Fresh green forsythia or pussy willow branches are cut and brought into the house as a symbol of spring and the renewal of life. Colored eggs and commercially or hand-decorated wooden eggs hang from these branches as a most attractive Easter greeting.

Parallel to the secular activities of holy week are the religious services. Various foods served on Holy Thursday and Good Friday reflect these somber days. A 'Speckkuchen' (bacon cake) and 'Grüne Sosse' (green sauce) are served in areas of Hesse as well as in other states on 'Grün Donnerstag'. In local circles these dishes are also served. Spinach and dumplings are other popular dishes.

Other than performing one's necessary daily chores and going to one's place of business, there is little activity on Good Friday. It is a quiet time and in many homes there is no television all day but rather sacred music is heard. Church services are attended if at all possible, for this is, for many, a day of solemnity. In special observance of this holy day and the sacrifice of Jesus Christ, a fish is served in most homes including those of non-Catholic denomination.

Easter Sunday brings the message of the risen Lord and with it a rebirth and renewal. For many the traditional 'Osterspaziergang' (Easter stroll) is a highlight of the day and affords the first opportunity to spend time out-of-doors — to be in nature. It reminds some, too, of the famous German writer, Johann Wolfgang von Goethe who described so vividly in his famous work, FAUST, the emotions of Faust as he took a walk with his servant on Easter morning. In his dialog Faust describes nature in its period of conflict between winter and spring — the snow showers, and the lack of flowers; however, the citizens dressed in their colorful Easter finery present a festive and lively picture. He is happy to be in their midst. Even today many local Germans enjoy a walk after dinner and are drawn out into nature. This custom also gives children the opportunity to look for chocolate eggs on the path. Of course, the Easter bunny has already hidden carefully dyed and decorated eggs in the garden or in the house. At the crack of dawn, children dash about to look for hidden treasures and fill their baskets (Eierlesen). There may also be contests of egg rolling (Eierschieben) to see whose egg will roll the farthest down a gentle slope or of balancing an egg on a spoon and running a specified distance.

In various sections of Germany other customs interfacing seasonal and religious celebrations occur. Easter fires, probably the survival of an old sacrificial rite which was later taken over by the Christian church indicate a symbolical burning of winter.

Water also plays a part in Easter observances. In Thuringia, the Harz and other districts of North Germany, the maidens or young unmarried girls dip up 'Easter water' from the river as the sun comes up, maintaining complete silence as they do so. This water is to make them beautiful, but the magic is lost if a word is spoken.

According to an ancient superstition, all church bells fly to Rome on the day before Easter. In the place of bells wooden clappers were used. Processions of boys with such clappers can still be seen in some villages in Baden. There are also other ancient traditions observed on Palm Sunday and during the Passion in Germany. One of these is the old dramatic representations of the Passion of Jesus, from which the internationally famous Oberammergau Passion Play developed.

Special dishes belong to Easter dinner observances in many places. Dinner is a very festive meal which in numerous homes consists of lamb, in others, ham or young goat. Pretzels of all sorts are made in some areas. One kind is an especially large and thick pretzel into which colored eggs in the shell are baked! Breads and braids of a yeast dough with raisins and nuts are also baked. Some of these are decorated with Easter eggs. A specialty in some homes is the 'Osterlamm' (Easter lamb) cake. 'It is baked in a lamb cake form and decorated with a fluffy white frosting and coconut simulating wool. Frequently the resurrection banner of a purple cross on a white background adorns the top of the cake. Upon returning from the late afternoon walk, the hostess may serve this cake and other special tortes with coffee to her hungry family and friends.

The joyous message of Easter truly brings with it a reawakening in nature and a renewal in man.

GRÜNE SOSSE
(Green Sauce)

Heli Fink

A classic sauce for Spring and Lent makes use of herbs; at least seven of them! This is a favorite dish in Frankfurt and Hessen and is often served with hot boiled potatoes.

- 1 lb. (454 gr) cottage cheese or farmer's cheese
- 1 pint (475 ml) sour cream
- 3 hard boiled eggs, diced
  - sugar and vinegar, to taste

Mix well and add very finely chopped herbs: dill, chives, dock, watercress, burnet, lemon balm, borage. Other greens that may be used or substituted are: parsley, basil, chervil, spinach. Amounts to taste.

Serves 4.

SPINAT UND SPIEGELEI
(Spinach and fried egg)

Hilde Cox

Even if my husband will never understand how anyone can eat such a combination, this is what you get in my house on "Gründonnerstag" (Holy Thursday or 'Green' Thursday):

1 or 2 packages (10 oz. frozen) chopped or creamed spinach (or one of each)
one fried egg, sunnyside up, per serving
small boiled potatoes

Cook spinach according to package instructions. Serve spinach on plates, place egg on top. Serve with small boiled potatoes. Be sure to have a nice, large cake for dessert!

SPECKKUCHEN
(Bacon Cake)

Hilde Cox

- 1 lb. (4 cups or 454 gr) flour
- 1 package dry yeast
- 1 teaspoon sugar
- 2 tablespoons oil
- 1 cup (¼ liter) milk
- ½ teaspoon salt
- 1 lb. (454 gr) bacon,
  - finely diced and rendered
- 1 teaspoon caraway seeds

Make a yeast dough from the first 6 ingredients, similar to pizza dough. Knead well. Let rise. Roll out on a greased cookie sheet or pizza pan, sprinkle with caraway seeds and bacon bits. Bake in very hot oven for 20 minutes.

FORELLE BLAU

Hilde Cox

(Blue Trout)

A simple and festive dish for Good Friday. The traditional fish in Franconia is carp.

8½ cups (2 liters) water	2 sprigs parsley
½ cup (118 ml) white wine	2 teaspoons salt
2 slices of lemon	10 peppercorns
2 small carrots, cut up	

Boil stock for 20 minutes to reduce liquid. Gently put in one trout per person, simmer for 8 to 10 minutes. Do not over-cook. Have warmed plates ready with small, boiled potatoes. Arrange trout curved on each plate, garnish with lemon slices and parsley. Serve with melted butter and a green salad.

Note: If you clean your own trouts, handle them with wet hands on a smooth surface, leave head and tail on the fish, clean insides. On a fresh trout, the skin will turn blue. In some German restaurants, where Blue Trout is a specialty, the guests can select a live trout right from a tank inside the restaurant.

HEFEKLÖSSE

Betty Straub

(Yeast Dumplings)

3½ cups (400 gr) flour	1 package dry yeast
1 teaspoon salt	¼ cup (59 ml) warm water (dissolve
rind of 1 lemon	yeast)
2 tablespoons melted butter	1 cup (237 ml) milk
	3-4 tablespoons sugar

Mix everything together in a bowl. Cover and permit it to rise in a warm place about 30-45 minutes. Then knead dough well and shape it into 6 to 8 one-inch balls, cover and let it rise again. After the balls have risen in 30-40 minutes, drop 3-4 dumplings into a large kettle filled ¾ full of boiling salted water. Cover pot tightly and cook for 15 minutes. Then take dumplings out onto a platter. With two forks tear them in half and put hot browned butter over it.

Serve with cooked dried mixed fruit (prunes, pears, apple rings or apricots). Cook them the night before with a slice of lemon. In my family this was usually eaten on Good Friday.

Serves 6-8.

BAUERNFRÜHSTÜCK

Gardy Epp

(Farmer's Breakfast)

4 medium potatoes	2 eggs
2 tablespoons butter or margarine	1 tablespoon milk
3 slices bacon, diced	1 tablespoon parsley, chopped

Peel the potatoes and cut them into very thin slices. Slightly fry the bacon in the butter before adding the potatoes. Reduce the heat, cover and cook for about 20 minutes, stirring occasionally. Then remove the cover and increase the heat to brown the potatoes. Stir the eggs and milk together and pour over the potatoes. Continue frying until the eggs are done. Sprinkle with parsley and serve.

Serves 4.

OSTERKRONE

Eva Maria Janetka

(Easter Bread)

My Nana, Josephine Monastero, traditionally baked this bread for the family at Easter. The colored eggs look like jewels on a crown!

1 cup (237 ml) cream	Egg glaze:
¾ cup (150 gr) sugar	1 beaten egg white with
½ cup (100 gr) butter	1 tablespoon milk
½ teaspoon salt	
2 packages active dry yeast	Decoration:
5-5½ (575-630 gr) flour	4 or 5 raw eggs and same
4 beaten eggs	number of hard cooked
2 teaspoons vanilla	colored eggs
2 tablespoons grated lemon rind	

In a small saucepan, scald cream. Add sugar, butter and salt and stir until butter melts. Set mixture aside in pan until lukewarm. Combine yeast and 1½ cups flour in a large bowl and gradually add cream mixture. Beat with a wisk until smooth and add beaten eggs, vanilla, lemon rind and 1 cup flour. Beat again with a spoon, add in 1½ - 2 cups flour to make a soft dough. Knead on a floured counter. Let rise in a greased bowl until twice its original size. Punch down and let rest 5 minutes. Divide 3 ways and roll into ropes about 26" long. Braid on greased baking sheet. Pinch ends to form ring. Grease eggs and press into dough. Cover and let rise until twice or double its size. Remove eggs. Brush eggs with glaze. Replace eggs and bake at 350° F. for 35 minutes. Remove eggs. Cool. Replace with colored eggs. This makes a colorful centerpiece for Easter breakfast and it's delicious! (The non-colored eggs used in the baking process can be used for salads or in recipes requiring hard-boiled eggs).

OSTERBREZEN

Udda Anderson

(Easter pretzels)

Boil and color eggs. Make basic yeast dough (any good or favorite recipe) sweetened. Let rise and punch down according to recipe. Form pretzels, press eggs into two openings of pretzels.

Bake according to yeast recipe. Cool and cover with a simple water/powdered sugar icing.

HEFEZOPF

Elisabeth Kottenhahn

(Yeast Braid)

Excellent freshly baked for hungry people - serve with coffee and whipped cream!

2¼ cups (½ liter) hot milk	1 tablespoon oil
¾ cup (150 gr) sugar	3 packages dry yeast
2 sticks butter	8 cups (910 gr) flour
2 eggs	

Mix all ingredients in this order in a bowl and knead well. Then cover airtight - no air should escape - and let rise for ¾ hour. Shape into desired form and put into cold oven. Set temperature at 340° and bake for ¾ hour. Brush with egg yolk before baking; add raisins if desirable or decorate with glaze and slivered almonds.

BRÖTCHEN

Elisabeth Kottenhahn

(Rolls)

2 cups plus 2 tablespoons (250 gr) flour	1 tablespoon sugar
½ cup (⅛ liter) milk	1 tablespoon melted butter
1 package (20 gr) dry yeast	1 tablespoon salt

Sift flour. Dissolve yeast in lukewarm milk, with the sugar added. When the yeast has foamed, add all other ingredients and beat into smooth dough. Form even-sized rolls and set aside to rise until double. Make a cut with a sharp knife down the middle, brush with egg yolk and bake to golden color in 350° oven for 20 minutes. (Use only good quality flour).

OSTERLAMMKUCHEN

Elly Gilgenast

(Easter Lamb Cake)

2¼ cups (260 gr) sifted flour	2 eggs
2¼ teaspoons baking powder	1 cup (200 gr) sugar
¼ teaspoon salt	¾ cup (178 ml) milk
½ cup (114 gr) oleo	

Sift four, measure, add baking powder and salt and sift again. Cream oleo, add sugar gradually and cream together until light and fluffy. Add eggs, one at a time, beating thoroughly after each. Add flour, alternately with milk, a small amount at a time, beating after each addition until smooth. Add vanilla. Pour batter into face half of lamb mold which has been thoroughly greased and floured. Round the batter slightly in regions of head and neck. Insert a toothpick in nose for added reinforcement. Cover with back side of mold (also greased and floured). Wire mold together. Place mold face down on a baking sheet and bake in hot oven (450°) for 15 minutes. Reduce heat to 350° and bake 45 min. longer. Remove from oven and open, taking off back side of form first. Allow cake to cool in face of mold for 5 min. Then loosen from sides of mold and remove very carefully. Set lamb upright on cake rack to cool.

Frosting

Scald 2 tablespoons milk. Melt 1 tablespoon oleo in it. Pour milk and oleo over 1½ cups (120 gr) confectioners' sugar, add ⅛ teaspoon salt and 1 teaspoon vanilla. This is a white fudge-type icing and will give the lamb a life-like look. You may also use a 7 minute icing for a fluffy look. Decorate with raisins or cloves for eyes and nose and red candy mouth, plus blue ribbon with little bell around neck. Place on platter, scatter coconut around with jelly eggs if desired. If desired, sprinkle coconut all over frosting for wooly effect.

ZIMT HEFE SCHNECKEN

Nancy C. McFadden

(Cinnamon Buns)

I can remember visiting my grandmother, Anna Schneider, when I was a little girl and sitting in her warm and cozy kitchen to enjoy her cinnamon buns with a glass of milk. Whenever she visited us she would bring a batch of her buns; later she gave me my first lesson in baking this family favorite. My grandmother was such a wonderful person who loved God and showed this in all that she did. Before the dough was covered to rise she would always make the sign of the cross on the dough, as though this was her "Thank you, God"! Now the fourth generation enjoys making grandmother Schneider's buns. My children love the aroma of these buns baking and it gives them a special feeling to know that their grandmother and great-grandmother baked them for their families too. My daughter bakes them at Christmas time and gives them as gifts to her friends.

2 packages yeast	Icing:
1¼ cups (275 gr) sugar	confectioner's sugar
1 13-oz. (390 ml) can evaporated milk	milk
1 13-oz. (390 ml) can water	approximately 1 teaspoon
¾ cup (170 gr) shortening	vanilla
8 - 10 cups (920-1150 gr) flour	
2 eggs	
1 teaspoon salt	
nuts and raisins - optional	
mixture of cinnamon and sugar	
butter or margarine (about 1½ sticks)	

Put 2 packages of yeast in about 3/4 cup (178 ml) of lukewarm water — set aside. Put ½ cup (100 gr) sugar in large pot; add can of evaporated milk and can of water; scald and then set aside to cool. Melt 3/4 cup shortening and set aside to cool. Sift enough flour (about 1 cup) into the cooled milk to make a sloppy dough; add the dissolved yeast mixture and let stand (covered) for ½ hour or until it starts to bubble. Beat 2 eggs and blend into bubbly dough; add melted shortening, ¾ cups sugar; and 1 teaspoon salt. Add enough flour (about 8-9 cups) to stiffen (not too stiff) — then knead a few times. Put dough into greased bowl; cover and let rise until dough doubles in bulk (about 1 ½ hours). When dough has doubled, punch it down and divide into 3 portions; roll out each portion, top with butter (or margarine), sugar and cinnamon mixture (nuts or raisins, if desired); roll up and slice, and place on greased pan or muffin tins. Cover and let rise again until double in bulk. Bake at 350°F. until golden brown. Cool. Ice with icing of confectioner's sugar, milk and vanilla. (Consistency of icing should be thick; add just enough milk to the confectioner's sugar to make a smooth, thick icing.)

ZIMT - NUSSKUCHEN

Erika Schirm

(Cinnamon Nut Coffee Cake)

Use ½ recipe rich yeast dough
2 tablespoons butter, melted
¼ cup (55 gr) sugar
½ teaspoon cinnamon
½ cup (120 ml) finely chopped toasted almonds

1 recipe icing (1 cup (130 gr) powdered sugar, 1 teaspoon hot water,
2 tablespoons butter)
   or
½ cup (40 gr) powdered sugar, 1-2 tablespoons lemon juice

Prepare dough in 12 x 12 inch square, shape with rolling pin. Brush with melted butter. Sprinkle with sugar and cinnamon. Sprinkle with almonds without stretching dough, fold over to within ½" of opposite side. Press edges together, place on greased baking sheet. Cover, let rise (1 hr.). Bake at 375° for 12 to 15 min. or till golden brown. Cool. Frost with icing.

NUSSTORTE

Eugenia Slavov

(Nut Torte)

7 oz. (200 gr) grated nuts
7 egg whites and yolks
2¼ cups (180 gr) powder sugar
⅓ cup (50 gr) Zwieback crumbs

2 tablespoons instant coffee
2 tablespoons rum
Filling:
whipped cream (or vanilla creme)
2 oz. (50 gr) grated nuts
2 tablespoons powder sugar

Beat egg yolks and sugar for 20 minutes to a foamy consistency. Add nuts, Zwieback crumbs which have been soaked in rum, and ground coffee beans. Add the stiffly beaten egg whites to this mixture. Pour into a cake pan (spring form) which is greased, dusted with flour and lined with wax paper. Bake 45 minutes at 350° - 375°. After cake has cooled, cut into two layers. Fill center with a filling of whipped cream or vanilla creme, nuts and sugar. Spread a sugar icing over the entire cake.

GEFÜLLTER KRANZ

Elly Gilgenast

(Coffee Ring)

2 lbs. or 8 cups (920 gr) flour	2 packages dry yeast
1 cup (200 gr) sugar	grated rind of one lemon
½ lb. (227 gr) butter or margarine	¾ cup (180 ml) raisins
2 eggs	¾ cup (180 ml) currants
cinnamon	1 cup (120 gr) chopped almonds
1 pint (474 ml) milk	1 teaspoon salt

Dissolve yeast in lukewarm milk to which ½ teaspoon sugar is added. Mix half of the flour, milk and one egg with the yeast and let it rise in a warm place. Then add the rest of the flour, the other egg, milk, soft butter, salt and ⅓ of the sugar. Let it rise again. Then roll out dough to a half finger thickness. Brush with butter. Add the other ingredients: raisins, lemon rind, currants, cinnamon, sugar, and almonds. Roll dough up, put onto greased baking sheet forming a ring. Brush with butter and sprinkle with almonds. Bake 1 hour at 350°. Cover with a thin sugar (powder) icing.

PROPHETENKUCHEN

Hilde Bredenbröcker

(Cake of the Prophets)

2 whole eggs	2 tablespoons cognac (brandy)
2 egg yolks	flour
½ cup (75 gr) confectioner's sugar	lemon juice
¼ cup (50 gr) butter	

Beat eggs with sugar until creamy. Add melted hot butter and brandy. Sift flour and add as much as can be stirred into the batter. Let rest in the refrigerator overnight.

Roll dough onto greased cookie sheet ¼ inch thick. Bake in 400° oven. Dough will look like hills and valleys (where the prophets walk). Immediately brush cake with melted butter, dust with confectioner's sugar and sprinkle with lemon juice. Cut into squares while still warm. (Use only fresh eggs. Cake will keep well stored in refrigerator.)

BAUMKUCHEN

Margot Traeger

(Tree Cake)

The name Baumkuchen applies, because the lighter and browner shades of the dough resemble the growth rings of a tree.

¾ lb. or 3 sticks (350 gr) butter or margarine	
1 ⅔ cups (350 gr) sugar	1¼ cups (150 gr) cornstarch
6 eggs	½ cup (⅛ liter) milk
1¾ cups (200 gr) flour	4 tablespoons apricot liquor

Glaze:

2½ tablespoons (35 gr) coconut fat (Crisco)
  5 tablespoons water   2 cups (250 gr) confectioner's sugar
  5 tablespoons (40 gr) cocoa   slivered almonds

Mix butter until light and creamy. Add sugar gradually; add apricot liquor. Beat eggs in one at a time. Mix well. Grease an 8 inch loaf pan. Spread a thin layer of dough in the bottom and bake under the broiler until golden brown (5-8 minutes). Spread another thin layer on top of this dough and broil again (5 minutes). Repeat this 18-20 times. There is no danger of burning the cake on the bottom since only heat from the broiler is used. After the entire cake is finished, place it on a wire rack.

For the glaze, mix melted Crisco with water and sifted cocoa and confectioner's sugar. Spread all over the cake and decorate with slivered almonds.

FRANKFURTER KRANZ   Beatrix Tannian
(Frankfurt Wreath)

This is an Americanized version of a very popular cake served in Germany.

Cake: 1 lemon cake mix

Prepare cake according to directions, pour batter into ring (wreath), mold or Bundt pan form. Bake according to directions. When cool, cut cake in half. Spread half of butter cream filling between layers. Spread other half over entire cake. Sprinkle Krokant on top and sides of cake. Refrigerate for several hours before serving.

Butter Cream Filling:
1 3-oz. package vanilla pudding (not instant) prepared with 2 cups (474 ml) milk,
1 cup (200 gr) sweet butter (unsalted — do not substitute margarine)

Prepare pudding according to directions and stir occasionally while cooling so no skin forms on top. Beat butter until fluffy. Add pudding slowly when temperature of pudding is the same as the butter in order to avoid curdling of butter.

Krokant or Praline topping:
1 tablespoon butter
2 tablespoons sugar
½ cup (100 gr) blanched, chopped almonds or chopped filberts

Melt butter, add sugar and heat until sugar is light brown. Add nuts and allow to brown slightly. Pour mixture onto a buttered or oiled flat plate. Allow to cool. When cold, slide mixture from plate and break up into small pieces.

HIMMELFAHRT, PFINGSTEN, TAG DER ARBEIT
(Ascension Day, Pentecost, Labor Day)
and
Hot Summer Days

The religious feast days of 'Himmelfahrt' (Ascension) and 'Pfingsten' (Pentecost) as well as the first of May, Labor Day, are all celebrated as legal holidays. Originally Ascension Day, celebrated 40 days after Easter, was a traditional time for men to go on outings together via bus, car or foot. Today, however, it is celebrated in some areas as Father's Day and more often as a family outing day. Mother's Day, which falls on the second Sunday in May, has had a strong commercial influence on setting aside a day for father. The commercialized bonanza of gifts for mother, however, still exceeds those for father.

Fifty days after Easter is Pentecost commemorating the descent of the Holy Spirit upon the disciples after Christ's ascension. Confirmation services are celebrated on this date in many Lutheran churches. This holiday also brings an extended vacation or break from school and is often celebrated with family excursions or longer trips. The milder weather encourages hikes, swimming, picnics, and any activity that takes one into the country or the mountains. The customs are similar to our own Memorial Day activities, which tend to announce the advent of summertime.

May Day is celebrated in a variety of ways depending upon the region.

In some areas there are gatherings of workers who hold rallies, give speeches and mark the day as an international worker day. In other areas one still experiences the setting up of a Maypole and the traditional dance around it. Former rural May customs evolved around winning a partner and involved activities for boys and girls of marriageable age. With the fast pace of an industrialized society, however, only remnants of these customs survive and are often continued today as an attraction for the large numbers of tourists.

The Germans' love for nature takes him 'ins Grüne', to the out-of-doors for hikes, outings or an afternoon stroll. Local Germans enjoy hiking all day and returning with an honest hunger to the home of one of the group for a simple hot meal prepared ahead of time and heated quickly. Depending upon the length of the tour, a snack of breads, lunch meats and cheeses are also taken along in a knapsack.

When the hot, sultry days of summer arrive, there are fresh vegetables and fruits and refreshing drinks to whet the appetite. A beverage of raspberry juice or 'G' spritzten', a mixture of wine and seltzer water are cool to the palate. All kinds of fruit cakes such as apple, peach or plum are baked on a sheet pan and served with whipped cream. Blueberry cake is a special treat during this season and tastes especially good after family members scrambled around to pick the berries. Cottage cheese dishes and wine pudding for desserts are also light and refreshing.

Many a German meticulously cares for a garden filled with vegetables and fruits and a yard which displays a multi-assortment and color of flowers. The canning and freezing of foods fresh from the garden still occupy hours in the kitchen; however, the flavorable culinary delights on cold winter days make it all worthwhile. This is the time to begin placing alternate layers of favorite fruits covered with rum into a crock in preparation for the 'Rumtopf' (the rum pot), which is used during the Christmas holidays.

The garden flowers and window box displays not only offer a spectacular beauty to the outside, but serve as a lovely house decoration. Freshly cut flowers reflect the German's love for nature and beauty. Bouquets usually adorn many areas of the house and especially the coffee table. When invited to afternoon coffee, one can always be assured of pleasing the hostess with a 'Blumenstrauss', a bouquet of flowers. They may be presented as gifts for all occasions from the simple cornflower picked in the field or garden to the red rose (reserved only for a more intimate friend or loved one), or to a more exotic flower or plant depending on the nature of the event.

SOMMER-SINGEN

Brigette and Wolf Conrad

A Silesian custom remembered

On the third Sunday in June all children between the ages of four to twelve would dress up and carry a 3-4 foot long willow branch which is covered with colored crepe paper and called "der Sommerstecken". In groups of 2-5 they begin in the morning and go from house to house "Sommern" to bring in the summer. They then sing their songs, after which the landlady rewards them with candies, baked goods, etc. Typical summer songs include: "Sommer, Sommer, ich bin ein kleiner Pommer . . ." and "Rot-Gewand, rot Gewand schöne grüne Linden . . ." (summer, summer, I am a little Pommerian, and red garment, red garment, beautiful green linden tree). In very few cases where the landlord would refuse to give out any sweets, the youngsters would retaliate by singing loudly: "Hühnermist and Taubenmist, in dem Haus bekommst du nichts, ist es nicht 'ne Schande in dem grossen Lande - (chicken dirt and pigeon dirt, in that house you receive nothing; isn't it a pity in this large land.)

SÜSS-SAURE SOSSE FÜR SALAT
(Sweet-and-Sour Sauce for Salad)   Marni Stauffer

Fry 5 or 6 slices of bacon until crisp. Remove from pan. (I usually also take out most of the bacon grease — it depends upon taste). Add 2 to 3 cups (475-700 ml) of cold water (again it depends upon thickness of dressing desired). Mix ¾ cup (150 gr) sugar, 1 tablespoon flour, 2 or 3 eggs and beat well. Add 2 tablespoons vinegar and salt to taste. Add to skillet and cook the mixture over low heat stirring constantly until the dressing is thickened. Pour the hot dressing over salad greens, toss and serve immediately.

PARADIESKRAUT   Kris Jeter
(Paradise Cabbage)

Cabbage and two sauce recipes were included in my grandmother's 1912 handwritten cookbook.

Grate a head of cabbage and blanche it in salted water until soft. Make a roux by cooking together in a skillet 2-3 tablespoons fat and an equal amount of flour. Add 2-4 tablespoons of tomato paste, season with salt and pepper and add 2-3 teaspoons of sugar. Add to cabbage and cook together until thickenend.

RHEINISCHE SAUCE
(Rhine Sauce)

Mix 2 tablespoons mustard with 3 tablespoons oil. Add 3 tablespoons sugar and the juice of a lemon. Mix well; use for basting dark meats, especially game.

SIEBENLÖFFEL SAUCE
(Seven Spoon Sauce)

Use equal amounts of mustard, butter, egg yolk, vinegar, beefstock, wine, sugar. Beat everything in double boiler over hot water until thickenend.

SÜSS - SAUER KRAUT   Lilli Fricke
(Sweet-Sour Cabbage)

In a small amount of water cook 1 small cut up head of cabbage and 1 medium cut up onion. Add 2 medium sliced apples, ⅔ cup (150 gr) sugar, salt and pepper. Cook 1½ hours on low heat. Add 2 teaspoons vinegar about 10 minutes before serving.

SELLERIESCHEIBEN

Elisabeth Kottenhahn

(Hot Celeriac)

Slice a peeled and cooked celeriac root. Mix one beaten egg with salt, pepper and nutmeg. Dip slices in egg and fry golden in hot butter. Serve, sprinkle with lemon juice.

SELLERIESALAT

Hilde Cox

(Celeriac Salad)

Make a marinade with oil, vinegar, salt, pepper and the juice of the canned celeriac. Add slices; let stand. As a variation add heavy cream and mustard to dressing, or a little horseradish.

BAYRISCHER KRAUTSALAT

Regina Ross

(Bavarian Cabbage Salad)

1 small head of white cabbage	1 tablespoon wine vinegar
salt, pepper to taste	1 tablespoon salad oil
½ teaspoon caraway seeds	boiling water

Remove core from cabbage, shred thinly. Add 1 tablespoon of salt and caraway seeds. Pour boiling water over it so all the cabbage is covered. Put lid on bowl and let stand about 15 minutes. Drain most of the water, but not all, add vinegar, oil and more salt and pepper to taste. Mix well. Do not refrigerate before serving.

KARTOFFELSALAT

Deutsches Haus
University of Delaware

(Potato Salad)

This receipe has been served at numerous Haus functions and has become a favorite with various members.

3 lbs. potatoes	⅓ cup (80 ml) salad oil
¾ cup (178 ml) boullion soup	2 tablespoons vinegar
1 large onion	salt and pepper
4-6 bacon strips	

Wash and cook potatoes. Peel and mince onion. Cut bacon into ¼ inch lengths. Fry until crisp; drain. Peel potatoes; cut into ⅛ inch slices. Add bacon, onion, oil, vinegar and soup. Salt and pepper to taste. Marinate one hour.

Serves 10-12.

PRINKENAUER SALAT
Kris Jeter
(Prinkenauer Potato Salad)

Included in my grandmother's 1912 handwritten cookbook.

Slice 4-6 boiled potatoes; mix with 1 finely diced apple. Make a dressing with 1 tablespoon mustard, 2 raw egg yolks, 4 tablespoons oil, 4 tablespoons sour cream. Season with salt and pepper and a little sugar. Add 1-2 teaspoons wine vinegar to taste.

Serves 6.

SPARGEL TOAST DANIEL
Chef Uwe Blessman
(Asparagus Toast Daniel)

24 asparagus spears, steamed or boiled until tender
8 hard-boiled eggs, shelled and sliced
2 cups white sauce (directions follow)
4 slices French bread, toasted
4 slices Italian ham (prosciutto)
Parmesan cheese

White Sauce: Melt 4 tablespoons of butter over low heat. Add 4 tablespoons flour and cook for a few minutes, stirring until well blended. Slowly add 1 cup each of hot milk or cream and ½ cup asparagus liquid, Simmer 5 minutes. Season with salt, pepper, a few drops of lemon juice and dry sherry, if desired. Thin with more liquid if needed. Add sliced eggs to one cup of sauce. Dividing evenly, spread on toasted bread. Top each with a slice of ham and asparagus spears. Spoon remaining sauce over asparagus. Sprinkle with Parmesan cheese. Bake for 10 minutes at 375°.

Serves 4.

SPARGEL SUPPE
Chef Uwe Blessman
(Asparagus Soup)

1 lb. fresh asparagus
½ cup chopped celery
½ cup chopped onions
½ cup chopped carrots
4 tablespoons butter

3 tablespoons flour
6 cups veal or chicken stock
1 cup heavy cream or milk
salt and pepper to taste

Cut asparagus spears in half. Boil tips until tender-crisp and set aside. Saute celery, onions and carrots in butter. Add flour and cook for a few minutes. Cook vegetable mixture and remaining asparagus in stock for 1½ to 2 hours. Puree in blender or processor. Add cream and cooked asparagus tips and heat thoroughly before serving. Season to taste.

SAURE KIRSCHEN SUPPE
Roberta A. Mayer
(Sour Cherry Soup)

As remembered by my mother

- 1 quart (1.14 liters) fresh sour cherries
- 6 cups (1.4 liters) water
  sugar to taste (in the range of ¼ to ½ cup)
- 2 cinnamon sticks
- 1 lemon, sliced thin
  tapioca

Pit and wash the sour cherries. Gently simmer the cherries in the water, with the sugar, cinnamon and lemon until the cherries are tender. Taste and adjust the sweetness as desired. Thicken soup with tapioca as desired. Remove from stove and let soup cool. Refrigerate overnight. Remove cinnamon sticks and lemon just before serving the chilled soup.

ROTKRAUT
Leni Holzhauser
(Red Cabbage)

In a saucepan with a tight fitting cover saute 1 large onion, finely chopped, in 2 tablespoons butter or bacon drippings until it is tender but not brown. Stir in 2 apples, peeled, cored, and thinly sliced and cook the mixutre for a few minutes longer. Add 1 cup (237 ml) of water, ½ cup (118 ml) red wine vinegar, 2 tablespoons sugar, 1 bay leaf and 1 teaspoon salt, a dash of pepper and bring the mixture to a boil. Stir in a large head of red cabbage. shredded, and cover the pan tightly.
Cook the mixture over low heat, stirring occasionally, for 35 to 40 minutes. Shortly before serving, mix 1 tablespoon flour to a smooth paste with a little water and stir it into the cabbage mixture. Heat the mixture, stirring constantly, until it thickens slightly.

ROTKRAUT
Sophia Kopec
(Red Cabbage)

This is a recipe that I remember my mother made and is one that I have enjoyed in my family!

- 1 lb. (454 gr) red cabbage
- ¼ lb. (112 gr) goose fat
- ¾ lb. (336 gr) fresh apples (I prefer cooking apples like Macintosh)

Shred red cabbage and put into medium sized pot. Cut up apples and mix with cabbage. Add about ½ cup water, cover with lid and cook for 15 minutes. Add goose fat and 1 tablespoon salt and cook 30 minutes longer.

LEIPZIGER ALLERLEI
(Mixed Vegetables a la Leipzig)

Gardy Epp

¾ cup (113 gr) of each: fresh peas, baby carrots, asparagus, kohlrabi and cauliflower

½ cup (118 ml) water
salt
sugar

1 teaspoon cornstarch
1 tablespoon cold water
1 tablespoon chopped parsley

Wash the vegetables, peel and slice the kohlrabi and break the cauliflower into flowerets. In a saucepan melt the butter or margarine and cook the vegetables in it for a short time. Then add the water and cook until the vegetables are done. Add salt and sugar to taste. Mix the cornstarch and cold water together, stir into the vegetables and cook until thickened. Serve with chopped parsley sprinkled on top.

SCHNÜSCH
(Vegetable Chowder)

Anneliese Chase

We were introduced to this unusual but yummy dish, when we biked through the Angeln part of Schleswig Holstein staying with a friend. Her family have been farmers in the Angeln district for centuries (and they still are); this recipe has been part of their tradition and does not seem to be known in any other parts of Schleswig. It added to the flavor that we could just go into the farm garden and pick the pea pods shortly before they went into the pot. The contrast of the delicate, almost bland Schnüsch to that of the Schinken and Hering is really delightful.

2 cups (300 gr) for each: carrots, sliced
                            new potatoes, sliced
                            fresh, young peas

1½ teaspoons salt
1½ tablespoons butter
 3 cups (¾ liter) milk
 ½ cup fresh parsley, chopped finely
 4 slices Holsteiner Katenschinken (or any kind of smoked Schinken, a ham)
 4 filets of Matjes hering

Boil prepared potatoes, carrots and salt in water, add peas during last 10 minutes. Drain and keep warm in a serving bowl. Heat (don't boil) the milk with butter, pour over vegetables, add parsley, add a little sugar and salt to taste. Serve the Schnüsch in soup plates with the Schinken on a wooden board and the Hering on a small side plate.

KRAUT STRUDEL

Anna Marie Cowell

(Cabbage Strudel)

This was my husband's favorite dish!

2 nice heads of cabbage (about 5 lbs.)
salt

3 cups (345 gr) Ceresota or all-purpose flour

1 tablespoon lard or Crisco

1 teaspoon salt

1¼ cups lukewarm water

Grate the heads of cabbage, salt down and let stand about 1 hour. Press out and stew in lard or Crisco until cabbage is heated through; then let it cool.

Dough:

Mix flour, lard or Crisco, salt and warm water and let stand for ½ hour. Then pull out dough on table on top of a cloth. Place cabbage on dough and roll both ends into center and place into a greased baking pan and bake about ½ - ¾ hour until nice and brown in a 350° oven.

GEFÜLLTE KRAUTWICKEL

Elly Gilgenast

(Stuffed Cabbage Rolls)

12 large cabbage leaves
boiling water
salt

2 beef bouillon cubes

1½ lbs. (680 gr) ground beef

⅓ cup (50 gr) bread crumbs

1 small onion, minced

¼ cup chopped fresh parsley

1 egg, slightly beaten

¼ teaspoon pepper

Place cabbage leaves overlapping in shallow dish and cover with boiling salted water. Let stand 5 minutes or until leaves are slightly wilted. Drain on paper towel. Trim coarse part of center (rib) of each leaf. Dissolve 1 bouillon cube in ¼ cup boiling water, cool. In mixing bowl mix thoroughly beef, bread crumbs, bouillon, onion, parsley, egg, 1 teaspoon salt and pepper. Divide mixture into 12 even portions and center one on each cabbage leaf. Fold sides over meat and roll up to make package. Place rolls seam sides down in 13 x 9 x 2 inch baking dish. Dissolve remaining bouillon cube in 1 cup boiling water and pour over rolls. Cover and bake in 375° oven for 45 minutes or until tender.

Makes 6 servings.

MAULTASCHEN

(Meat Filled Noodles)

Sylvia M. Arles

Broth:
> soup bones
> celery (2 stalks)
> water to cover everything

Simmer for 1 hour, then remove bones and celery. Strain; add 3 beef bouillon cubes and simmer until dissolved. Pepper and salt to taste; set aside.

Meat filling:

2 lbs. (900 gr.) ground beef	1 teaspoon paprika
3 eggs	¼ teaspoon nutmeg
soft bread crumbs (2 slices of bread)	2 tablespoons parsley flakes
1 teaspoon pepper	1 large onion, chopped, sauteed

Mix together and set aside in refrigerator.

Noodle dough:

3½-4 cups (400-460 gr.) flour	4 eggs
½ teaspoon salt	cold water

Mix first three ingredients and knead, slowly adding water until dough is smooth. Add more flour until dough comes off side of bowl. Knead dough for one minute on floured countertop. Divide into two. Roll dough until very thin. Be sure to flour countertop often to keep dough from sticking to it. Spread half of meat mixture over half of dough and fold other half over. Seal openings by pressing ends of dough together. To form two inch squares use a wooden cooking spoon and press the handle firmly into dough. Cut out the squares and cook in boiling salted water. Repeat with other half of noodle dough and meat mixture. Serve in hot broth garnished with some parsley flakes.

Serves 6-8 persons.

HÜHNER - ODER KALBSFRIKASSEE

(Chicken or Veal Fricassee)

Ellen Stixrude

Cover meat of choice with water, add 1-2 sliced carrots, salt and cook for approximately 2 hours. Take out the meat and keep warm. Add 1 tablespoon butter to soup and thicken with flour. Add a little lemon juice. Beat 2 egg yolks, remove soup from heat and stir eggs carefully into soup. Return meat to soup and serve with rice or potatoes.

HÜHNER FRIKASSEE

Grace Strohmann

(Chicken Fricassee)

Mother always had this on Sunday especially when we had company for dinner.

Alma M. DeMott

1 large stewing hen	1 teaspoon whole allspice
(cut into serving pieces)	1 teaspoon mustard seed
1 medium onion	½ cup (100 gr) celery - cut up
2 bay leaves	½ cup (120 ml) barley
1 teaspoon whole cloves	salt and pepper to taste

Cover chicken with water. Simmer about 2 hours, then add ½ cup of well-washed barley and simmer another two hours or until barley is soft and the chicken nice and tender.

KALBSFRIKASSEE

Edith Dommert

(Veal Fricassee)

1 package (10 oz.) of six patty shells, frozen

1 lb. (454 gr) veal	3 tablespoons flour
2 cups (475 ml) water	1 cup (237 ml) veal stock, strained
1 carrot, sliced	1 can (8 oz.) mushrooms, drained
1 stalk celery, diced	1 can (8 oz.) cut asparagus, drained
1 clove	1 tablespoon white wine
1 small bay leaf	drops of lemon juice
salt and pepper	salt and white pepper
3 tablespoons butter	1 egg yolk, beaten

Prepare patty shells according to package directions.

Put veal in saucepan, add water and bring slowly to a boil. Skim carefully. Add carrot, celery, clove, bay leaf, salt and pepper. Cover and simmer slowly for 25-30 minutes or until veal is done. Strain stock and cut meat in bite-size pieces.

Prepare thick sauce by melting butter in saucepan, stir in flour, add veal stock slowly. Cook and stir continually over moderate heat until boiling and cooked to desired thickness. Add mushrooms and asparagus, season carefully with white wine, lemon juice drops, salt and pepper. Warm until just heated through. Stir egg yolk into sauce. Spoon into warm patty shells and serve.

SCHINKENHÖRNCHEN

Lizzy Haenlein

(Ham-filled pockets)

If prepared in a larger size this is a good cold weather meal and is served as a main meal. Prepared in a smaller size they can be used as an appetizer or also eaten as a complement to soup.

Dough:

4 cups (450 gr) flour	16 oz. (450 gr) cottage cheese
1⅓ cups (300 gr) butter	pinch salt

Blend all ingredients together and cool in refrigerator ½ hour. Roll out on board to knife thickness and cut out with a large oval cutter (half moon shape).

Filling:

11 oz. (300 gr) ham or lean bacon	caraway seed
3 tablespoons onions, chopped	1 egg for decoration
3 tablespoons parsley, chopped	thin with milk
3 tablespoons sour cream	2 pinches of salt

Roast filling ingredients together, cool and add cream. Use cooked ham as in small cubes but saute onions. Note: lean hamburger can be substituted. Put filling into dough cut outs, brush edges with water to seal. Bake at 400° for 20-25 minutes on the bottom rack.

BERLINER LEBER
Gardy Epp
(Fried Liver with onions and apples)

1 lb. (454 gr) beef liver, sliced	2 onions, sliced thinly
flour	2 apples, cored and sliced
6 tablespoons butter	

Wash the liver, pat dry, turn in flour and fry in hot butter until browned on both sides. Remove the liver to a serving platter, salt and pepper and keep warm. In the same butter fry the onion slices for one minute, then add the apple slices and fry another minute. Spoon this mixture over the liver with all the butter from the skillet and serve immediately.

BERLINER KALBSLEBER
Ruth Bischoff
(Calves Liver)

liver	tomatoes
onions	mushrooms

Wash liver and remove any skin tissue or sinews with a sharp knife. When using beef or pork liver place it for ½ hour in a bowl of milk for added tenderness. Pat dry, dip into flour. Heat fat (shortening) in a heavy frying pan; when hot, add liver and fry at a moderate heat. At the same time add sliced onions and mushrooms on the side of the meat and saute to a golden brown. Add sliced tomatoes and fry until tender. Turn liver and fry until tender. Turn liver and fry on both sides about 5-7 minutes all together. Remove to a heated platter, salt and arrange onion, mushroom, tomato mixture on top of liver. This tastes good served with mashed potatoes or an apple-potato mixture called 'Heaven and Earth'.

HIMMEL UND ERDE
(Heaven and Earth)

Add warmed applesauce to mashed potatoes. Season with sugar, salt, vinegar for a sweet-sour taste. Before serving pour melted butter over this.

LEBERKNÖDEL
(Liver dumplings)

Elli Beck

12 oz. (336 gr) liver	2-3 tablespoons flour
4 oz. (113 gr) ground beef	1 onion
1 Kaiser roll,	1 egg
soak in water, then squeeze out	salt and pepper

Chop liver and mix with other ingredients.
Form small dumplings (1 inch in diameter) and drop into boiling salt water and simmer about 10-15 minutes.

LEBERKNÖDEL
(Liver dumplings)

Regina Ross

4 small rolls or	2 eggs
5 slices white bread (stale)	1 teaspoon salt
½ cup (118 ml) milk	generous pinch of majoram
¾ lb. (336 gr) beef liver	grated rind of 1 lemon
1 small diced onion	1 tablespoon flour
	breadcrumbs as needed

Pour milk over diced bread and let soak in. Squeeze out excess milk. In food processor or meat grinder grind bread, liver and onion together. Mix in eggs, salt, marjoram and lemon rind. Add flour and breadcrumbs, a little at a time, until mixture can be shaped into dumplings.
Wet hands to do the shaping. Drop into big pot of boiling water and let simmer 25 to 30 minutes.
Serve with beef broth; sprinkle with chopped chives.

Makes 7-8 dumplings

KÖNIGSBERGER KLOPSE
(Meatballs in caper sauce)

Ingeborg Keith

Meatballs:

1 lb. (454 gr) ground beef	¼ cup (59 ml) milk
¼ lb. (113 gr) ground veal (optional)	1 teaspoon salt
1 egg	¼ teaspoon pepper
1 cup (150 gr) breadcrumbs	1 onion

Saute chopped onion in 2 tablespoons butter. Add to rest of ingredients and mix thoroughly. Shape into balls about 2" in diameter. Bring to boil in saucepan: 3 cups water, 2 tablespoons chopped onion and 1 bay leaf, 1 clove, 2 pepper corns, ¼ teaspoon salt. Put meatballs into the liquid. Bring to boiling, reduce heat and simmer 20 minutes. Remove meatballs and set aside to keep warm. Strain the liquid. Heat in saucepan 2 tablespoons butter, blend in 2 tablespoons flour. Gradually add 2 cups of the liquid, a little lemon juice and 1 tablespoon chopped capers. Bring to a rapid boil, stirring constantly. Return the meatballs to the sauce and heat thoroughly. Serve with butter noodles or boiled potatoes.

KÖNIGSBERGER KLOPSE
(Meatballs)   Edith Fischer

For the meatballs:
- 1¾ lbs. (790 gr) ground meat, mixture of beef and pork
- 9 slices white bread, stale, with crusts removed
- 2 cups (450 gr) cooked, grated potatoes
- 5 anchovy fillets
- 2 eggs
- 1 level tablespoon flour
- ⅜ level teaspoon salt
- 2 tablespoons capers
- a dash of pepper

For the sauce:
- 3 rounded tablespoons butter
- 2 rounded tablespoons flour
- 3 tablespoons capers
- 4 cups (950 ml) soup stock
- 1½ teaspoons lemon juice
- ½ rounded teaspoon salt
- pepper

Soak bread in water about 2 minutes, then squeeze out. Mince anchovies as fine as possible. Blend meat, bread, potatoes, minced anchovies, eggs, flour, salt, pepper, and capers together well. Form eighteen balls about the size of small eggs (3 per person). Roll balls in flour and drop in a large deep pot of medium boiling salted water for 12 minutes. Remove and keep warm.

Melt butter in a large pot with cover. Add flour and blend well with fork. Do not brown. Add capers, lemon juice, salt and pepper. Add boiling soup stock. Stir well with a fork or egg whisk to prevent lumps. Simmer slowly, covered, for 15 minutes, stirring frequently to prevent burning. Add meatballs to sauce and simmer for 5 minutes. Serve with boiled potatoes, vegetables.

KÖNIGSBERGER KLOPSE Elnora (Toots) Schweiger
(Meatballs)

In a large bowl put

1 cup (150 gr) soft breat crumbs
¼ cup (59 ml) milk
1 medium onion, chopped

Heat in skillet:

2 tablespoons butter. Add onion and cook over medium heat until golden. Add this to the bowl with

1 lb. (454 gr) beef ground twice	1 egg beaten
¼ lb. (112 gr) veal ground twice	1 teaspoon salt
4 anchovy fillets, mashed	¼ teaspoon pepper

Combine lightly; shape into balls about 2 inches in diameter. Bring to boil in a large saucepan

3 cups (711 ml) water	1 whole clove
2 tablespoons chopped onion	4 peppercorns
1 bay leaf	

Carefully put meatballs into liquid, bring to boil; reduce heat and simmer 20 minutes. Remove balls and set aside to keep warm. Strain liquid. Heat in the saucepan 2 tablespoons butter; blend in 2 tablespoons flour. Heat until mixture bubbles. Remove from heat, gradually add 2 cups of the liquid and 2 tablespoons lemon juice and 1 tablespoon capers chopped. Bring rapidly to a boil stirring all the time. Cook 2 minutes longer. Return meatballs to sauce and heat. Serve with buttered noodles. (Anchovy fillets and capers may be omitted; however the flavor is very mild.)

KLOPSE MIT SAURER SAHNE Edith E. Yaeger
(German Meatballs with Sour Cream)

This recipe comes from East Prussia and is a favorite in my family.

1½ lbs. (680 gr) beef and pork, mixed
About 3 * slices of white bread soaked in 2 eggs and enough milk to moisten.
Add to meat: small onion (chopped), parsley, salt, pepper (to taste) and a little diced celery.

Form into small balls.
Simmer ½ cup (118 ml) water and ½ cup (118 ml) mild vinegar and 1 bay leaf in a skillet for about 10 minutes.
Add the meatballs and cook about 20 minutes, turning several times. Remove balls from skillet.
Thicken the sauce with a little flour, ⅓ cup (80 ml) sour cream, a little sugar; put the balls back into the sauce, and let cook for 5 minutes. **

* - Use more if you want to stretch the meat further.
** - (Optional) After you put balls back into sauce, you may add about one tablespoon imported capers to give extra flavor.

66

LABSKAUS

Helga Melton

Dieses Gericht ist an Bord beheimatet, wird aber auch gern an Land gegessen. Zu seiner Herstellung muss Smutje Kurs durch sämtliche "Proviantlasten" nehmen. Nicht umsonst heisst es: "Im Labskaus findet der Seemann alles wieder, was er das letzte Jahr über verloren hat".

Die Zutaten bestehen aus:

1 kg gekochtem Pökelfleisch	6 Salzgurken
4 Matjesheringen	500 g roten Beeten
Zwiebeln	Fleischreste, Schwarten und Rindfleisch.

Das ganze wird durch den Wolf gedreht, mit 1½ kg Stampfkartoffeln zusammengemischt und gekocht, bis es gar ist. Dazu gibt es dann einen Rollmops und nun:
"Spitz an, Backschafter, hau rin, noch'n Schlag".

LABSKAUS A LA HELGA

Helga Melton

So wie der traditionelle Sauerbraten in unserem Haus als Alltagsgericht in Form von "Sauerbraten Meatballs" vereinfacht, bzw. amerikanisiert wurde, so ist es auch dem Labskaus ergangen.
Labskaus a la Helga, mein beliebtestes Schnellgericht, in 15 Min. auf dem Tisch and von Mann und Jungen gern gegessen:

Instant mashed potatoes für 4 Personen, nach Bedarf doppelte Menge

1 Dose Corned Beef	etwas Salzgurkenwasser
1 grosse Zwiebel	Salzgurken, rote Beete aus dem Glas
Margarine	4 Spiegeleier (statt Matjesheringe)

Feingehackte Zwiebel in Margarine goldgelb dünsten, eine Dose Corned Beef hinzufügen, mit etwas Gurkenwasser vermengen und erhitzen.
In der Zwischenzeit instant mashed potatoes nach Vorschrift zubereiten, dann das Corned Beef nur teilweise mit dem Kartoffelbrei vermengen, damit die Masse nicht eine unappetitlich rosa Farbe annimmt.
Auf einer grossen, vorgewärmten Platte anrichten, mit roten Beeten, Salzgurken und Spiegeleiern garnieren.
Dazu einen frischen, grünen Salat servieren.

The following two recipes are the English version.

LABSKAUS
(Sailor's Hash)

This dish, popular on the North Sea coast, is at home on board ship but is also popular on land. For its preparation the sailor makes his way through numerous provisions. Therefore, it is not without due reason that one hears the saying: "Im Labskaus findet der Seeman alles wieder, was er das letzte Jahr über verloren hat" (in the hash the sailor finds everything which he has lost in the past year).

- 2¼ lbs. (1 kg) cooked pickled meat
- 4 matjes herring
  onion
- 6 salt pickles
- 2¼ cups (500 gr) beets (pickled, chopped)
  meat leftovers, pork rind, beef

Grind everything through a meat grinder or food chopper, then mix with 3-4 cups (1½ kg) mashed potatoes and cook until done.
Serve with pickled herring and "Spitz an, Backschafter, hau rin, noch 'n Schlag" (Dig in, sailors, eat up!)

LABSKAUS A LA HELGA
(Helga's Hash)

I have Americanized this recipe and it has become my favorite speedy dish. I can prepare this in 15 minutes and my husband and sons enjoy eating it.

Instant mashed potatoes for 4 (2 cups or 500 gr); if desired, double
- 1 12 oz. can corned beef
- 1 large onion
  margarine
  salt pickles, salt pickle juice
- 1 16-oz. jar beets
- 4 eggs (fried - sunny side up - in place of matjes herring)

Saute finely diced onions in margarine until yellow, add 1 can corned beef, a little pickle juice, mix and heat through.
In the meantime prepare instant mashed potatoes according to instructions on package. Then gradually mix corned beef mixture with potatoes so that it doesn't become too bright red.
Place on a large, prewarmed platter and garnish with beets, pickles and fried eggs.
Serve a fresh leafy green salad with this.

PICKELSTEINER
(Stew)

Anne Braun

1½ lbs. (670 gr) potatoes (6 medium)
3-5 carrots
½ head of small white cabbage
2 stalks of leek
2 large onions
small bunch of fresh parsley

3-4 stalks of celery
1 lb. (454 gr) top round steak

All of these ingredients should be kept separately and cut finely into cubes or slices. Place in Dutch oven or other heavy covered cooking container, which has been greased with margarine. Put ingredients into container layer by layer, starting with meat. Sprinkle each layer with salt and pepper, not too freely, and on top of all this add one cup of Maggi's (or other) Instant Beef Bouillon. Simmer for at least one hour without stirring; keep tightly covered.

ERDBEERBLITZ TORTE
(Strawberry Blitz Torte)

Joan Schoenleber

Cake

Beat well yolks of 4 eggs (save whites for meringue)
½ cup (100 gr) sugar
½ cup (114 gr) soft butter
½ cup (58 gr) flour

3 tablespoons milk
1 teaspoon baking powder

Cream butter and sugar together. Sift together flour and baking powder and mix in alternately with milk. Spread on the bottom of two 8 inch greased pans. Bake with meringue on top.

Meringue
Beat 4 egg whites. When stiff, add 1 cup (200 gr) sugar. Spread on top of two layers and bake at 350°F for 25 minutes.

Custard Filling
½ cup (100 gr) sugar
⅓ cup (38 gr) flour
½ teaspoon salt
2 cups (474 ml) milk

4 egg yolks or 2 whole eggs, beaten
2 teaspoons vanilla
strawberries

Mix sugar, flour and salt into saucepan. Stir in milk. Cook, stirring until it boils. Boil one minute. Remove from heat. Stir a little more than half of mixture into egg yolks. Blend into hot mixture in saucepan. Bring to boil. Cook and blend in vanilla.
Put custard filling between layers and top with strawberries. Whipped cream may be substituted for custard filling.

SCHINKENNUDELN

Hilde Schwoegler

½-¾ Pfund Nudeln
180 g Schinken
    schwach ¼ 1 dicken sauren Rahm
    2 Essl. geriebenen Käse

wenig Salz
20 g Butter
    Weckmehl

Von den gekochten Nudeln legt man davon eine Lage in eine mit Butter gestrichene Auflaufform, darauf wenig Salz, die Hälfte Schinken, Rahm und Käse, dann Nudeln, die andere Hälfte Schinken, Rahm und Käse und die letzte Lage wieder Nudeln.

Man legt Butterstückchen darauf, bestreut den Auflauf leicht mit Weckmehl und lässt ihn ½ - ¾ Stunde bei 350° backen.

Oder man verschlägt 1-2 Eier mit ⅛ 1 Rahm oder Milch, gibt den gewiegten Schinken, Käse, Salz und Nudeln dazu, mengt alles leicht untereinander und füllt die Masse in eine leicht gefettete Auflaufform und backt wie oben.

KOPFSALAT

Hilde Schwoegler

2 Köpfe Salat
2-4 Essl. feines Öl
3-4 Essl. Essig oder
    Saft einer Zitrone

½ Teel. Salz,
    Prise Pfeffer
    nach Belieben Zucker
1 Teel. Schnittlauch

Von den Salatköpfen, welche möglichst fest sein sollen, werden die äusseren Blätter in 3-5 Teile geschnitten doch so, dass immer ein kleiner Teil von der Blattrippe mitgeschnitten wird. Die inneren Blätter werden in der Mitte durchgeschnitten, nur das Salatherz lässt man ganz. Sodann wäscht man den Salat in einer Schüssel mit reichlich Wasser und gibt ihn zum Abtopfen auf ein Sieb. Kurz vor Gebrauch kann man ihn in einem Salatkorb oder Serviette leicht hin-und herschwenken, damit alles Wasser gut herauskommt.

Der Salatbeiguss wird in einer Schüssel gut vermengt, nach Belieben etwas geriebene Zwiebel, oder noch besser die Schüssel mit einer Zwiebel oder Knoblauchzehe ausreiben, den Salat zugeben, leicht gemischt und sofort zu Tisch bringen.

Statt mit Öl kann der Salat auch mit Rahm angemacht werden, und man rechnet zu 3 Teil Rahm 1 Teil Essig oder Zitronensaft.

SCHINKENNUDELN
(Ham Noodle Souffle)

These recipes were favorites in my family. As soon as lettuce and greens appeared in the vegetable garden in the spring of the year, my mother made these Schinkennudeln and the Boston lettuce dishes. They were delicious and refreshing.

½-¾ lb. noodles
  6½ oz. (180 gr) ham, chopped, cooked
  1¼ cups (¼ liter) thick sour cream
  3 tablespoons grated cheese

a little salt
1¼ tablespoons (20 gr) butter
breadcrumbs

Cook noodles until tender in boiling water. Drain well. Place a layer of noodles into a greased souffle dish or casserole. Add a little salt, half of the ham, cream and cheese. Then layer again with noodles, then the ham, cream, cheese and noodles as the final layer. Dot with tiny pieces of butter and sprinkle lightly with breadcrumbs. Bake at 350° for 30-45 minutes.

Alternate Method

Cook noodles as directed above. Beat 1 or 2 eggs with ½ cup (⅛ liters) cream or milk. Add the ham, cheese, salt and noodles and mix everything lightly together. Place mixture into greased souffle dish and bake as above.

KOPFSALAT
(Boston Lettuce)

2 heads Boston lettuce (firm)
2-4 tablespoons olive oil or salad oil
3-4 tablespoons vinegar or lemon juice
  ½ teaspoon salt

pinch of pepper
sugar to taste
1 tablespoon chives

Prepare heads of lettuce by removing the exterior leaves and cutting them horizontally in 3-5 parts retaining a section of the vein of the leaf in each piece. Cut the interior leaves in half; do not cut up the lettuce heart. Wash the lettuce thoroughly in a large bowl filled with water and set into a sieve to drain. Before using, be sure to toss and drain all excess water.

For the salad dressing combine all of the above ingredients in a bowl and mix together. Prepare the salad bowl by rubbing it with an onion or garlic. Then place lettuce into bowl, pour dressing over lettuce and mix lightly. Serve immediately.

Option: Instead of oil, the dressing can be prepared with cream. In this case prepare 3 parts cream to 1 part vinegar or lemon juice.

BISKUITTEIG ZU TÖRTCHEN ODER OBSTKUCHEN
(Fruit-Tarts)

Gudrun McGee

3 eggs	¾ cup + 1 tablespoon (180 gr) sugar
3 tablespoons water	1⅓ cups (150 gr) flour

Mix egg yolks and water until smooth. Slowly add sugar and beat until foamy. Beat the egg whites and alternately mix flour and stiff egg whites into the foamy batter. Fill the batter into well-greased baking forms and bake at 350° for approximately 30 minutes. Cover the cold tarts with fresh strawberries (or other fruit) and cover the fruit with a glaze. I use the Dr. Oetker package glaze and follow instructions on the package.

KIRSCHTORTE
(Cherry Torte)

Kris Jeter

I found this recipe in a 1912 handwritten cookbook which belonged to my grandmother.

2 cups (½ lb. or 227 gr) flour	grated lemon peel
½ cup + 1 tablespoon (125 gr) butter	1 egg
½ cup (100 gr) sugar	1 hard boiled egg yolk
1 teaspoon vanilla	pitted cherries, as desired

Mix all ingredients. Butter a springform or cake pan and sprinkle with breadcrumbs, add dough evenly and bake in a moderate oven (350°F.) for ¾ hour. Add pitted cherries on top and bake for another ½ hour. Serve with whipped cream.

KIRSCHENMICHEL MIT SCHWARZBROT
(Cherrycake with rye bread)

Hilde Cox

- 6 eggs (medium) or 4 large
- ¾ cup (150 gr) sugar
- 1 cup (150 gr) rye breadcrumbs
- 2½ oz. (70 gr) unblanched ground almonds
- ½ glass red wine (¼ cup or 60 ml)
- 1 teaspoon cinnamon
- 5 teaspoons baking powder
  grated lemon peel
- 1 can (or as desired) drained Montmorenci cherries (sour cherries)

Moisten bread crumbs with red wine. Beat egg whites. Beat egg yolks with the sugar until thick and creamy. Add cinnamon, lemon and baking powder to egg yolk mixture. Add bread crumbs, almonds. Carefully add egg whites. Grease a 10″ springform pan, fill with batter, sprinkle cherries on top and bake 45 minutes at 325°F. Let cool; serve with whipped cream.

KIRSCHKUCHEN MIT GRIESS
Elisabeth Kottenhahn
(Cherrycake with Farina)

3¼ cups (¾ liter) milk
¾ cup (150 gr) farina
6-7 egg yolks
1 cup (200 gr) sugar
dash salt

½ cup (100 gr) butter
3½ oz. (100 gr) ground almonds
grated lemon rind of ½ a lemon
2 lb. (900 gr) cherries, pitted

Cook milk with farina; let cool. Add egg yolks. Cream butter and sugar, add to farina. Fold in stiff egg whites. Fill greased springform pan with batter, add cherries and bake in 340° oven until done.

RÜHRKUCHEN
Olga Fischer
(Basic cake with fruit topping)

¾ cup (150 gr) sugar
1 stick (113 gr) sweet oleo
3 eggs
1½ cups (175 gr) flour

2 teaspoons baking powder
1 teaspoon vanilla
2 tablespoons milk
fresh or canned fruit

Mix oleo, sugar, eggs. Add flour, vanilla, baking powder, milk and mix well. Place into a 10″ round buttered baking pan. Place any fresh or canned (drained) fruit on top. Sprinkle with vanilla sugar. Bake at 350° for 30 - 40 minutes.

BLAUBEEREN KUCHEN
Elaine Gilgenast
(Blueberry Cake)

This is a recipe that I obtained from my mother-in-law. I always enjoyed eating a piece of her blueberry cake and now bake it for my family.

½ cup (113 gr) butter
2 eggs
4 teaspoons baking powder
2½ cups (290 gr) flour

½ cup (100 gr) sugar
½ cup (118 ml) milk
2½ cups (600 ml) berries

Flour berries well. Blend butter and sugar; beat in eggs, add sifted dry ingredients with milk. Fold in berries. Place into a 9 x 15 greased pan. Sprinkle top with sugar and bake at 400° for 20 minutes and then at 375° for approximately 25 minutes.

RHABARBERTORTE
(Rhubarb Pie)

Leni Holzhauser

2 cups (474 ml) cut rhubarb	2 tablespoons flour
1 cup (200 gr) sugar	1 tablespoon water
1 egg	grated rind of 1 small lemon

Have the pie crust rolled and fitted into pie pan. Mix together all the ingredients listed. Fill the pie pan and lattice the top with strips of dough. Place in hot oven and then reduce the heat to bake the filling thoroughly.

Pie crust:

1½ cups (175 gr) flour	pinch of salt
½ cup (113 gr) crisco	3-4 tablespoons ice water

Mix all ingredients together until dough forms a ball. Divide the dough, use half for bottom and the rest for lattice on top of pie filling.

ZWETSCHGENDATSCHI
(Plum Tart)

Regina Ross

Ingredients are for dough covering one cookie sheet 17¼ x 11½ x 1 or two 9" cake tins and lattice on top.

Pastry dough:

2¾ cups (320 gr) flour	1¾ sticks (200 gr) of butter
¾ cup (150 gr) sugar	3-4 lbs. (1350-1800 gr) small purple plums*
1 teaspoon baking powder	⅓ cup (66 gr) sugar
pinch of salt	
2 eggs	* apples (McIntosh) can be used instead

Preheat oven to 425°F.
Combine dry ingredients, add eggs and diced, cold butter and knead into dough (butter has to be completely worked in.) Cover and refrigerate. Wash and dry plums, remove stones and cut into quarters.
Flour dough ball and roll out on cookie sheet or on wax paper, about ¼" thick, sides up about 1". Fit plums tightly onto dough. Bake in preheated 425° oven on lower third level for 15 minutes. Sprinkle ⅓ cup sugar over plums, lower heat to 400° and bake 15 more minutes. Let cool before cutting. Can be frozen and reheated, or thawed at room temperature.

ZWETSCHGENKUCHEN

Ursel Kroll

(Plum Cake on a sheet)

This is a very popular cake recipe in my family!

- 6 tablespoons (90 gr) butter or margarine
- ½ cup (100 gr) sugar
- 1 egg
  salt
- 2 cups (230 gr) sifted flour
- 1 level teaspoon Dr. Oetker's baking powder
- ¾ cup (178 ml) milk (approx.)
- 2 lbs. (900 gr) purple plums - fresh or frozen, halved and stoned

Cream butter and slowly add sugar and egg. Mix baking powder with flour and add by the spoonful to the butter mixture, alternating with the milk. Use only enough milk to make a heavy dough that drops from the spoon quite slowly. Spread dough on a greased cookie sheet (with a rim) and top with plums, cut side up.

Bake at 400°F. for 40 minutes. Remove from oven and sprinkle with sugar. After cake cools, cut into squares.

TORTENBODEN

Elli Beck

(Sponge cake for torte)

6 eggs	1½ teaspoon baking powder
1 cup (200 gr) sugar	3 tablespoons warm water
1 cup (115 gr) flour	

Beat eggs, sugar, and water, sift flour and baking powder. Add to egg mixture. Pour into greased springform and bake at 350° about 40 minutes.

STREUSEL

Ruth Olivier

(Crumbs)

This crumb mixture is simple and easy to use on a plain cake dough (yellow sheet cake) as well as over a fruit sheet cake.

Melt 6 tablespoons butter, add ½ cup (100 gr) sugar and stir in 4 heaping tablespoons flour with a fork. Use hand to scatter over dough. This is enough for a 9-inch pan.

QUARKKUCHEN

Annelies B. Menta

(Cottage Cheese Cake)

Dough:

1¾ cups (200 gr) flour	1 egg
6 tablespoons (84 gr) butter	3 tablespoons sour cream
7 tablespoons (84 gr) sugar	

Sift flour on board, form well in center, add sugar, eggs, and sour cream. Cut butter into small pieces and place around flour. Swiftly combine all ingredients with hands. Let dough rest in refrigerator for one hour.

Filling:

2 cups (474 ml) cottage cheese, dry	1 cup (100 gr) flour
¾ cup (168 gr) sugar	2 tablespoons melted butter
5 eggs, separated	4 tablespoons raisins
rind of 1 lemon	2 tablespoons ground almonds

Blend cottage cheese until smooth. In bowl mix cottage cheese with sugar, beaten egg yolks, and lemon rind. Add sifted flour and melted butter. Beat egg whites very stiff and fold carefully into mixture. Place dough into greased springform. Sprinkle with raisins, add cottage cheese mixture, smooth surface with spatula. Sprinkle ground almonds on top and dot with a little butter.

Bake at 375° for about 45 minutes. Before taking cake out of pan, loosen edges of cake from springform to prevent cake from falling. Let cool, dust with confectioner's sugar.

QUARKKUCHEN

Leni Holzhauser

(Refrigerator Cheese Cake)

2 tablespoons granulated gelatin (Knox)	2 cups (474 ml) cottage cheese
½ cup (118 ml) water	1 tablespoon grated lemon rind
1 teaspoon salt	¼ cup (60 ml) lemon juice
½ cup (100 gr) sugar	1 teaspoon vanilla extract
1 tablespoon cornstarch	2 stiffly beaten egg whites
½ cup (118 ml) milk	1 cup (237 ml) heavy whipped cream
2 egg yolks slightly beaten	

Soften gelatin in cold water about 5 minutes. Combine salt, sugar, cornstarch and add to milk in top of double boiler and stir until sugar is dissolved. Add egg yolks to milk mixture. Cook in double boiler stirring constantly until mixture thickens.

Remove from heat, add gelatin to mixture and set aside to cool. Add cottage cheese which has been put through a sieve, lemon rind and juice and vanilla extract. Fold in stiffly beaten egg whites and whipped cream. Pour into heat resistant glass dish lined with Zwieback crust. Then sprinkle top of cake with remainder of crust. Chill.

Pie Crust:

2 cups (300 gr) fine Zwieback crumbs (or 1 box Zwieback)
1 teaspoon cinnamon   ⅓ cup (66 gr) sugar
¼ teaspoon salt   ⅓ cup (80 gr) butter or margarine

Mix all crust ingredients together in the order given. Pat mixture evenly into heat resistant glass pie plate saving ⅓ for topping. Put in refrigerator for at least 2 hours to chill and set. Add cheese cake filling.

QUARKTORTE
(Cottage Cheese Torte)

Annelies B. Menta

Whenever I visit my girl friend in East Germany, she serves this delicious cheese cake which is a favorite in her family and is fast becoming a favorite in ours.

Dough:

1⅔ cups (200 gr) flour   1 tablespoon baking powder
⅓ cup (85 gr) sugar   1 stick plus 1 tablespoon (130 gr)
1 large egg   margarine or butter

Filling:

3 cups (672 gr) dry cottage cheese   1 tablespoon flour
2 cups vanilla pudding,   sugar to taste
    cooked and cooled   lemon rind + juice of 1 lemon
3 egg yolks   3 egg whites

To prepare dough:

Sift flour and baking powder on board, form well in center, add sugar and egg. Cut butter into small pieces and place around flour. Swiftly combine all ingredients with hands. Let dough rest in refrigerator for one hour.

For topping combine all ingredients except egg whites. Beat egg whites until very stiff and fold carefully into cottage cheese pudding mixture.

Place dough into greased springform pan and pour filling over it. Bake at 375°F. for 45 minutes. After cake has cooled, cover surface carefully with chocolate icing.

Chocolate icing:

3 tablespoons confectioner's sugar   2 tablespoons condensed milk
3 tablespoons cacao   ¼ cup (60 gr) shortening, melted
1 egg

Combine sugar and cacao, add egg, milk and melted shortening. Mix until very smooth and spread on cake.

VANILLECREME
Martha Heinemann

½ 1 Milch oder Rahm
1 Stange Vanille

3-5 Eigelb
120 g Zucker

Die Milch wird mit der durchschnittenen Vanilleschote unter Schlagen langsam zum Kochen gebracht. Unterdessen rührt man Zucker und Eigelb schaumig, gibt die durchgesiebte lauwarme Milch zu, schlägt die Masse auf dem Ofen, bis sie steigt, giesst sie in eine Schale und lässt die Creme erkalten.

VANILLECREME
(Vanilla Creme)

2 cups (½ liter) milk or cream
1 vanilla bean

3-5 egg yolks
½ cup (120 gr) sugar

Bring milk slowly to a boil. Add grated vanilla bean beating constantly. Beat egg yolks with sugar until frothy. Add the lukewarm milk mixture to this and beat the mixture vigorously on the stove until it reaches boiling point (do not boil.) Pour into a bowl and allow to cool.

VANILLESOSSE
(Vanilla Sauce)

Maria Wiedemann

1 cup (¼ liter) milk
1½ teaspoons (5 gr) cornstarch
1 tablespoon (10 gr) salt

2 tablespoons (20 gr) sugar
2 eggs
½ vanilla bean

Stir all ingredients together and set in top of double boiler. Stir constantly until mixture thickens. Then set pot into cold water and continue to stir constantly until mixture cools and is smooth.

WEINCREME
(Wine Creme)

Elisabeth Kottenhahn

This is a refreshing dessert especially after a full course dinner on holidays!

1½ packages unflavored gelatine
3 eggs
½ cup (⅛ liter) boiling water

1 cup (¼ liter) good white wine
⅓ cup (75 gr) sugar
2 tablespoons lemon juice

Dissolve gelatin in hot water, set aside to cool. In double boiler over hot water, beat egg yolks with wine until foamy. Add sugar. Beat continuously with wire whisk until mixture thickens. Add lemon juice and gradually add gelatin. Beat egg whites until soft peaks form; add a little sugar. Fold into cooled egg yolk mixture. Fill into glass bowl or individual dessert glasses and refrigerate.

WEIN SOSSE
Lia Wycoff

(Wine sauce)

Sift together into the top of double boiler
  1 cup (200 gr) sugar
  2 tablespoons cornstarch
  ¼ teaspoon salt
Add, stirring well
  2 cups (474 ml) boiling water

Stirring gently and constantly, bring mixture to a rapid boil over direct heat and cook for 3 minutes. Place over simmering water. Cover and cook about 12 minutes, stirring 3 or 4 times. Vigorously stir about 3 tablespoons of the hot mixture into
  1 egg yolk, slightly beaten
Immediately blend into mixture in double boiler. Cover, cook 1 minute. Remove cover and cook 2-4 more minutes. Stir slowly to keep mixture cooking evenly. Remove from heat and blend in
  ¼ cup (57 gr) butter
  2 teaspoons vanilla extract
Cool sauce and add gradually, stirring in
  ½ cup (118 ml) white wine
Serve over steamed dumplings.

ZITRONENCREME
Maria Wiedemann

(Lemon Creme)

1½ lemons (juice)	½ cup (⅛ liter) white wine or water
4 eggs, separated	1 package unflavored gelatin
⅔ cup (125 gr) sugar	

Beat egg yolks with sugar until dissolved and foamy. Set aside. Dissolve gelatin in hot water or wine and set aside to cool. Add to egg mixture and beat until mixture begins to thicken. Fold in stiffly beaten egg whites, gently but thoroughly. Turn into a serving bowl or individual dessert glasses. Chill until set. Serve with vanilla sauce if desired.

RHABARBERAUFLAUF

Maria Wiedemann

(Rhubarb Souffle)

⅔ cup (75 gr) flour
¾ cup (75 gr) almonds, blanched and grated
5 tablespoons (75 gr) butter
⅓ cup (75 gr) sugar

5 eggs, separated
½ cup (⅛ liter) milk
grated rind of 1 lemon
rhubarb compote

Mix butter and milk and bring to boil. Add flour gradually, beating constantly over low flame until mixture loosens self from sides of pot. Then add egg yolks, sugar, and grated lemon rind. Fold in stiffly beaten egg whites gently but thoroughly.

Butter a souffle or Gugelhupf pan and put ½ of mixture into pan. Add rhubarb compote (not too thin) over mixture and then cover this with ½ of the souffle mixture. Bake ½ hour at 350°.

ZWETSCHGENRÖSTER

Leni Holzhauser

(Rum-laced stewed plums)

1 cup (200 gr) sugar
¾ cup (178 ml) water
2 lbs. (900 gr) small blue Italica plums

cinnamon stick
dark rum to taste

In a heavy saucepan bring 1 cup sugar and ¾ cup water to a boil and simmer to syrup for 5 minutes. Add 2 lbs. small blue Italica plums, pitted, and a 1-inch piece cinnamon stick. Simmer the plums for about 10 minutes or until they are very soft. Remove the pan from the heat and stir in dark rum to taste. Cover the pan and let the plums cool. Serve them with Kaiserschmarren.

ROTE GRÜTZE

Alice Pietschmann

(Red Fruit Pudding)

This was always a welcomed dish on hot days and I remember my mother making it frequently. My children and grandchildren love it too, so I have continued the tradition in my family.

I use berries that are available in season:
raspberries and gooseberries,
blueberries and rhubarb, or
blackberries and currants

Cook a combination of 2 berries or fruits and bring to a boil. When cooked, rub through a fine sieve, cheesecloth or in a blender to a puree.

To 5 cups (1180 ml) of juice add ¾ cup (145 gr) of farina (or cream of wheat) and simmer for 3-4 minutes. Stir constantly. Chill for several hours. Serve plain or with cold milk as a dessert or a cool lunch when it's too hot to eat much.

GRIEßSCHMARREN
Eugenia Slavov
(Farina pudding)

2 cups (½ liter) milk	2 tablespoons (25 gr) sugar
½ cup (100 gr) butter	2 tablespoons (30 gr) sugar (for final sprinkling)
salt	4 tablespoons (50 gr) farina

Bring milk to boil; add salt and stir in farina. Cook until mixture thickens. Heat butter in a pan, add the farina mixture and let stand in oven for 1 hour. Then break up mixture with a fork. Sprinkle with sugar and serve with a fruit juice.

RHABARBERKOMPOTT
Magda Ruoff
(Stewed Rhubarb)

rhubarb
sugar
lemon or orange rind

Whatever rhubarb weighs, add ¼ of that weight in sugar, after you wash and clean rhubarb and cut into 2 inch pieces. Let sit and draw juice for one hour, then add ¼ cup water and some lemon or orange rind. Cook very slowly at low heat until soft or tender.

RUMTOPF
Annelies Menta
(Rum and Fruit Crock)

It takes time and patience but it is well worth the effort! Start in June with fresh strawberries.

Clean a tall crock, fill in the cleaned strawberries (16 oz. or 454 gr) with 1 cup (200 gr) sugar. Pour a bottle of good rum (100 proof) over the berries. Cover crock and place in cool place.

Every month add another 16 oz. (454 gr) fruit with 1 cup (200 gr) sugar each time - e.g. raspberries, cherries with pit, peaches, apricots, plums, pears (peel and slice) and pineapple.

If necessary, add more rum. The fruits have to be covered with rum all the time. When all fruits are in the pot, let it rest for 4 weeks. On the first of **Advent the Rumtopf is ready.** The liquid can be drunk straight or with champagne added. The fruit tastes especially good as a topping on pudding or ice cream.

"Zerbrichlich schuf den Topf der Schöpfer
Drum wird allzeit blühn die Zunft der
Töpfe!"

(The maker created the pot (ceramic) so that it can break
Therefore the guild of the ceramic artesian will flourish forever!)

PFIRSICH BOWLE
(About the Peach 'Bowle' Punch)

Wendall Friday

I received this recipe from colleagues in the Ruhr area of Germany while on a business trip there. I enjoyed it so much that they sent me the recipe and I have been serving it for years. When friends come over for an evening of conversation I have made this and have served semi-sweet cookies with it. One could also serve cheese and crackers.

According to an old instruction to gourmets a peachbowle should always be prepared by tender hands and only be served to attentive and appreciative drinkers. In any case, however, a peachbowle should be made by tender hands. It may be served for meals, however dishes like potato dumplings and roast pork are not exactly suitable; much better is fine poultry, like pheasant or fish, such as trout.

Essential for the preparation of a bowle is that one starts in time. The notion that for the preparation of the bowle inferior wines may be used, is absolutely wrong. No strong wines should be used, it is true, but nevertheless good light kinds which should if possible have so much natural sweetness, that only a small amount of sugar has to be added. In any case the mixing with mineral water or soda is forbidden. Concerning the temperature of the drink it may be said that bowles should be served comparatively cool, approximately 50°F. On hot days one will serve it cooler, on cool days a little warmer. No ice should be put into the bowle itself, however, and also not into the glasses. Therefore it is recommended to cool the glass from the outside or, if one can use only big glasses, not to fill them up to the top.

For the preparation of approximately 3 liters of bowle about 2 liters light good white wine (according to personal taste; I prefer Mosel wine) and one bottle of good champagne (1 liter) are necessary. For this amount of wine one needs about 10-12 ripe peaches. (They should be very ripe and soft to touch.) These are cleanly peeled approximately 8-10 hours before the bowle is supposed to be served. Then the fruits are divided into six parts, the stone is carefully removed, and the flesh close to the stone cut off. (I cube the peaches to an approximate ⅝ inch size.) These peach pieces are put into a **porcelain or glass bowl, each layer sugared** (not too much) **and already** soaked with about ¼ liter of the wine. The bowl is covered well and stored away to a cool place, so that the fruit will not turn brown. (Make sure that all peach parts are under the wine; then refrigerate.)

One hour before the bowle is supposed to be served, one places the fruits and the juice in the bowl into the big Bowle bowl and adds the rest of the wine. Now about 2 liters of wine are in the bowl. Immediately before the bowle is served, the champagne is added. In any case it should be avoided that the fruits while they are prepared and used for the bowle should come into contact with metal. This is also valid for the bowl itself. The fruits should not be cut with a steel knife. Of course, the ladle may be metal-preferably silver. However, it should not stay in the Bowle bowl after the glasses have been filled, but be put onto a plate beside the bowl.

It should be emphasized that one does not make a fine bowle if concentrated alcohol like cognac, gin, whiskey, or liqueur is added to make it stronger. These drinks taste better when they are pure. The bowle serves 12-14 people. Well, then 'Prosit'!

HERBST FESTE
(Autumn Fairs and Festivals)

The beginning of September and the autumn season brings a new bustle of activity with the opening of school and the harvesting of crops. Wide-eyed and bashful first graders march off to school with the traditional 'Schultüte' (school bag), a large cone-shaped cardboard container filled with pencils, pens, candies and cookies. This is to help make the first day and the beginning of school a little sweeter. Some local Germans have continued this tradition throughout the elementary school years of their children.

Jahrmärkte (yearly markets), Kirmes (fair), Vereinsfeste (club festivals) and the Oktoberfest take place in the smallest village to the largest city. Club festivals include the singing and folk-dancing clubs that celebrate an anniversary in the spring or fall. The Kirmes, a type of country fair, is especially popular in many smaller villages and offers numerous types of amusements and entertainment for all ages. Such markets and fairs last from two or three days to one week.

Wine festivals abound in the Rhine and Moselle regions as well as in other areas where wine is cultivated. Street dancing, singing and drinking of the 'Heurigen' (new wine) dominate the village scene. More and more festivals are becoming popular as communities and local tourist agencies attempt to attract tourists to participate in their folklore events. More commercial interests may be observed today along with the numerous traditional fairs and local customs.

The 'Schützenfest' (marksmen festival) is one of the oldest traditions

84

in which sharpshooters, organized in clubs, demonstrate their skills. The competition culminates in the selection of a 'Schützenkönig' (king) and/or Schützenkönigin (queen). The best marksman reigns supreme for one year. Along with the volleys of firing in the competition shooting there are the usual activities of eating, drinking and merrymaking that are popular at all festivals.

The largest 'Volksfest' (folk festival) of all is the Oktoberfest, celebrated in late September and early October on the 'Theresienwiese' (Therese's Meadow) in the heart of Munich. The Oktoberfest originated in honor of the wedding of Crown Prince Ludwig to 'Princess Therese von Sachsen Hildburghausen in the year 1810. A horse race and public festival were held to which horsemen and guests from all over Bavaria were invited. The celebrating continued for several days. Since this festival was such an enjoyable success, it was repeated the following year and was expanded to include agricultural exhibits in order to give more impetus to agriculture and the harvest. As a result of these festivities, traditions and customs have continued throughout the years and today this fest attracts guests from all over the world. On the opening Saturday the beautifully decorated wagons representing the seven breweries are drawn by four and six horse teams. These horses represent the finest of the beer steeds. On Sunday the festival parade with costumed members of Alpine groups and shooting societies march through the city to the fair grounds.

Each year this festival has become more commercial and more expensive; however, this fact does not deter the spirits of the thousands of merrymaking guests who flock to the 'Wiese'. The consumption of beer and food is staggering. Grilled chicken, varieties of sausages, barbecued pork, giant pretzels as well as the 'Weisswurst' (white sausage), a specialty of Munich, are enthusiastically consumed along with liters of beer. All of this along with parades, dances in the traditional costumes, music and general congeniality blend into a high-spirited 'Gemütlichkeit' which lasts for fourteen to sixteen days.

For the farmer this autumn season is the culmination of his toil and he is thankful when his crops produce a bountiful harvest. Religious and secular customs abound in the joyful celebrations and communal entertainment. Everyone joins the farmer in expressing gratitude through dance and merrymaking activities. Often today the original significance of a particular fest is lost; however, most autumn activities originate from traditions of giving thanks for the harvest.

A festival well-known in the Alpine regions is the bringing down of the cattle from the mountains. After spending the summer grazing on the lofty meadows and producing milk for numerous dairy products, the decorated and prize-winning animals are returned to their stalls in the villages below.

Although the Germans do not celebrate the thanksgiving feast to which we are accustomed, the Protestant church usually celebrates an Erntedankfest (harvest thanksgiving) on the first Sunday in October; in Catholic areas the date varies according to the church district. While the churches decorate their altars with the harvest produce and lay-people place food, flowers and farm implements before the altar, prayers and songs of thanksgiving acknowledge the blessings of the season. Symbols of fertility are seen in the 'Strohpuppe' (straw doll) and the 'Erntekrone' (harvest crown).The latter which serves as a decoration in the house is usually a crown of plaited straw or several ears of corn displayed on the front door. These decorations may also hang in a conspicuous place until the first Sunday in Advent.

The bounty of the harvest brings a joy of autumn dishes. With the new wine an onion cake (Zwiebelkuchen), freshly baked and warm from the oven is often served. The cooler autumn days introduce a desire for soups and more robust foods. Hunters try their aim at favorite game such as venison and rabbit. Roasts, fall vegetables, and apple dishes present further culinary delights.

Throughout the fall and winter months when the weather does not permit many outdoor activities, families and friends get together socially with good food and drink. The 'Stammtisch', (a table reserved for a special group), in local restaurants and locales becomes more popular again, the fall 'Kaffeeklatsch' is reactivated and the beginning of the theater and concert season adds a cultural flavor of activity. The shorter days move into the grey days of November and soon into the more festive events with the beginning of the Advent season.

ZWIEBELKUCHEN
(Onion Cake)   Emilie Toman

This is a well known recipe from my section of Germany - Württemberg. I make it often here and serve it as an appetizer. It's popular with all of my guests. It can be frozen too. Take from freezer and heat through. Serve hot.

Yeast Dough:
  2 cups (250 gr) flour (this should be somewhat warm)
  1 package yeast - dissolve in a little warm milk (¼ cup or 60 ml)
  4 tablespoons (50 gr) butter, softened
  3 egg yolks
  ½ cup (⅛ liter) warm milk

Put flour into bowl and add all ingredients. Mix together and work dough until smooth. Let dough rise for about 1 hour or more in a warm place. Roll out and put in a pie plate (or jelly roll tray). Let it rise for 1 hour again.

Filling:
  2 lbs. (900 gr) large onions (slice or cut into small rings)
  ⅛ lb. (54 gr) bacon, diced   ¼ teaspoon salt
  3 eggs   3 cups (700 ml) sour cream
  ½ cup (58 gr) flour   1 tablespoon caraway seeds

Saute onions in bacon. Beat eggs, add flour, salt, sour cream and caraway seeds. Stir into onion and bacon mixture. Put over top of dough and dot with butter. Bake in preheated oven at 375° for 30 minutes until dough is crisp and brown around edges.

ZWIEBELKUCHEN
Edith Stark
(Onion Cake)

This is a Thuringian recipe which my mother baked. It is similar to pizza.

2 cups (230 gr) flour	6-8 onions (or scallions)
½ teaspoon salt	½ cup (118 ml) cream of wheat
2 tablespoons shortening	(cooked and cooled)
½ envelope dry yeast	1-2 tablespoons caraway seeds
(dissolve in 3 tablespoons warm	4 slices bacon (diced) - fry
water and 1 teaspoon sugar)	slowly 3-4 minutes

Prepare yeast dough of first 4 ingredients. Place in a warm draft free area to rise. When it has risen, punch the dough, roll it out (about ¼" thickness) and place it on a buttered cookie sheet. Let stand. Prepare filling. Cut up onions and cook until soft. Separately cook cream of wheat according to directions and let cool. Be sure dough has an edge like a pie crust (not too thick). Fill onto dough the cream of wheat, then the steamed onions. On top add caraway seeds to taste and sprinkle cut up slightly fried bacon over entire surface. Let it rise again and bake at 375° for 20 - 25 minutes until golden crisp.

ZWIEBELKUCHEN
L. Burkhardt Salerno
(Onion Pie)

Pastry: (or your own pie shell)

2 cups (230 gr) sifted flour	¾ cup (170 gr) butter
1 teaspoon baking powder	1 egg, beaten
½ teaspoon salt	1 tablespoon cream

Filling:

4 large onions	½ cup (118 ml) heavy cream or milk
2-3 tablespoons butter	2 eggs, beaten
¼ teaspoon salt (to taste)	½ teaspoon caraway seeds
½ tablespoon flour	

Cook the onions in butter (large skillet) until very soft. Add salt and caraway seeds. Stir in flour, then slowly add cream. Remove from heat and add mixture of beaten eggs slowly. Pour into pie shell. Bake in a pre-heated oven at 375° until dough is done. Serve hot or cold.

BERLINER SCHUSTERJUNGEN
Helga Walters
(Shoemaker's Apprentices)

The shoemaker's apprentices had so much work that they only had time enough to eat 'salt rolls'. Salzkuchen are delicious with Schmalz, (lard) and Harzer Käse (Harz cheese).

Salzkuchen (Salt Rolls):
- 3½ cups (400 gr) rye flour
- 2¼ cups (200 gr) unbleached white flour
- 2 envelopes dry yeast
- 1½ cups (⅜ liter) water
- salt

Sift flour into bowl. Make a little dent in the middle of the flour and add broken up yeast pieces, add a little warm water and mix the yeast, flour and water slightly. Cover with towel and place in prewarmed oven for 15 to 20 minutes. When double, add in remaining water and the salt and work dough until shiny and elastic. Shape dough into small balls, press slightly down on them, and place them on floured cookie sheet. Let them rise until double in size in warm draft free place. Before baking dust them with flour. Bake for 15 to 20 minutes at 425° F.

KÄSE BLITZEN
Alma M. DeMott
(Quick Cheese Appetizers)

Mother served these with her before dinner glass of wine! They were done faster than lightening.

- 1 cup (115 gr) flour
- ¼ lb. (57 gr) butter
- 1 8-oz. package Shefford's snappy cheese (or any sharp cheese)

Rub butter and flour together. Mix in cheese. Roll out, cut with biscuit cutter; put under broiler a few minutes.

LEBERNOCKERLSUPPE
Magda Ruoff
(Liver Dumpling Soup)

3 eggs	1 small onion, finely chopped
6 tablespoons (90 gr) butter	salt and parsley to taste
¼ cup (40 gr) bread crumbs	2½ quarts (2 liters) beef or
3½ oz. (100 gr) liver	chicken stock

Remove skin and veins from liver. Grind. Stir butter until soft, add eggs at room temperature, add bread crumbs and mix well. Add finely chopped onion, parsley, salt and lastly, the liver. Refrigerate mixture for ½ hour. Then form small dumplings with two teaspoons and drop into boiling soup stock. Cook for 5 minutes.

MARKKLÖSSCHENSUPPE
(Marrow Dumpling Soup)

Magda Ruoff

1 oz. (28 gr) bone marrow	salt
1 egg	nutmeg
3 tablespoons (28 gr) bread crumbs	

Cook bone marrow with water and vegetables for a good stock. Mix bone marrow, egg, bread crumbs, salt and nutmeg together. Form little dumplings with two teaspoons and drop into boiling stock. Let simmer for 10 - 15 minutes.

KRAUTSUPPE
(Cabbage Soup)

Anna Herold

2 small heads cabbage, shredded	salt, pepper
fat, flour	fried sausage, sliced
2 quarts (1⅞ liters) soup stock	

Shred the cabbage and brown in a little hot fat. Sprinkle with a little flour, stir well and cook till the flour begins to brown. Pour boiling stock over the cabbage, season with salt and pepper and simmer for one hour. Before serving, add slices of fried sausage.

KARTOFFELSUPPE
(Potato Soup)

Elly Gilgenast

4 large potatoes, peeled and diced	½ cup minced parsley
1 large onion, diced	2 teaspoons salt
1 quart (950 ml) water	½ teaspoon pepper

Place all ingredients into large saucepan. Cook uncovered over moderate heat 40 - 45 minutes or until potatoes are soft, stirring occasionally. With wooden spoon press some potatoes against sides and bottom of pan to break into small pieces.
Makes about 2 quarts.

KARTOFFELSUPPE
(Potato Soup)
Annemarie Rawe

1½ lbs. (6 medium) potatoes	2 carrots
1-2 onions, chopped	4-6 cups (950-1400 ml) beef stock
1 leek	2 oz. (50 gr) bacon (4 slices) chopped
1 stick celery	salt and pepper

Peel, wash and dice potatoes and carrots. Clean and slice celery and leek. Add these vegetables to the simmering beef stock. Cook until soft, then put through a food mill. In a frying pan saute bacon and onions until lightly browned; add to the soup. Garnish with chopped chives or parsley. Serve with croutons.

Leek is rich in vitamin B and C and has very few calories. This soup is considered very healthy for stomach sickness (without the bacon).

ERBSENSUPPE
(Split-Pea Soup)
Elly Gilgenast

ham hock and soup bone	2 carrots, chopped
1 lb. (454 gr) green split peas	3 ribs celery, chopped
1 onion, chopped	salt and pepper

Put bones into large kettle with peas, onion, carrots, and celery and 2 quarts water. Bring to boil, cover and simmer, stirring occasionally, 1 - 1½ hrs. until peas become mushy. Remove meat from hock and add to soup. Season with salt and pepper to taste.

ERBSENSUPPE MIT KNACKWURST
(Green Split Pea Soup with Knockwurst)
Pauline Zistl

My grandchildren love this green split pea soup which is my own recipe.

2 quarts (1⅞ liters) water	salt & sage to taste
1½ cups (340 gr) green split peas	2 tablespoons butter or margarine
1 large onion	1-2 tablespoons flour
4-5 carrots	2 beef bouillon cubes
5 stalks of celery with leaves	

Cut up all vegetables and cook with the split peas until soft. Strain liquid and all ingredients through sieve/grinder. Then melt the butter or margarine, add flour and let simmer briefly. Add the strained vegetables and liquid and bouillon cubes. Let simmer for 15 - 20 minutes. Add slices of knockwurst and serve.

FRISCHE SUPPE MIT KLÖSSEN

(Fresh Soup with Dumplings)   Ellen Stixrude

As soon as the weather turns cold my family enjoys eating this soup.

Place beef into cold water, add salt, pepper and bay leaf and simmer for about ¾ hour. Add celery leaves, sliced carrots, parsnip (a little) and simmer. Make little meatballs from lean ground beef. Add salt, pepper, minced onions, breadcrumbs (if necessary for binding), and roll balls into the size of a walnut (¾ inch). Take out the celery leaves and meat, add meatballs to the simmering soup and cook about 10 minutes. The meatballs will rise to the top when done. Prepare rice. The meat can be cut up and added to the soup or served as a side dish with potatoes and horseradish sauce for those with big appetites. To prepare horseradish sauce take as much liquid from soup as necessary. Add a tablespoon butter and thicken with flour. Add horseradish to taste. Approximate cooking time for soup is 2 hours. Before serving soup, sprinkle finely chopped parsley over the soup.

UDDAS UNGARISCHE GULYASSUPPE

(Udda's Goulash Soup)   Udda Anderson

A hearty dish which is a favorite after the concert, theater or after an evening of drinking. It is a popular 'midnight snack' which is frequently served before the drive home.

1 lb. (454 gr) meat (part beef, part pork) cubed
  same volume (or slightly more) of diced onions
5 cloves of garlic, diced
3 grated carrots
2 lbs. (900 gr) peeled fresh or canned tomatoes, cubed
4 bay leaves
  a good dash of caraway seeds
2 teaspoons thyme
2 tablespoons paprika
1 lemon rind, grated
1½ cups (355 ml) heavy cream

Fry meat until golden brown. Add all ingredients up to and including thyme. Add enough liquid (dry red wine, chicken broth*, water or a mixture of these) to almost cover the meat and onion mixture. Simmer over low flame until meat is tender (add liquid if necessary). Add paprika, a pinch of sugar (or honey), the grated yellow part of a lemon rind. Add salt to taste and 1½ cups of heavy cream. Stir, warm, but do not bring to boil.
Serve with fresh crusty white bread. Add a tossed salad and you have a full meal. Yum-m-m.

*Chicken broth can be made with bouillon cubes.

GULYASSUPPE
(Goulash Soup)

Regina Ross

To be at its best this soup should be made at least one day before it is served. It is delicious served late in the evening after the theater or concert and especially on cold evenings.

1½ lbs. (680 gr) beef chuck (or other stewing meat)

3 tablespoons butter	2 tablespoons tomato paste
3 strips diced bacon	1 teaspoon caraway seeds
2 large onions, diced	½ teaspoon marjoram
1 heaping tablespoon sweet paprika	2 quarts (1⅞ liters) water
1 teaspoon salt (more later, to taste) pepper	(substitute part of it with beef broth, if possible)
2 tablespoons wine vinegar	3 medium size potatoes, peeled and diced

Cut beef into ½ to 1 inch cubes. In a large saucepan, sauté onions with 2 tablespoons butter and diced bacon until medium brown. Add paprika, stir well and set aside. Set a heavy, large frying pan over high heat and brown the beef with the remaining butter quickly. Do not crowd the beef into pan, or it will not brown. It's better to use two pans or do it in two steps. Add browned beef to sauteed onions. Pour some of the 2 quarts of liquid into the frying pan and scrape off pan juices. Reserve. Put saucepan back on high heat, stir beef and onions together, add all other ingredients, liquid and pan juices last, except potatoes. Bring to a boil, cover and simmer 1¼ hours. Add diced potatoes and cook slowly 15 to 20 minutes longer. Crush a few of the potatoes with a fork to thicken soup. Add more salt, if necessary.

4-6 servings.

LEBERKÄSE
(Hot Liver Pâté)

Annelore Schmidt

This dish has been prepared with great success to the delight of family and guests!

1 lb. 2oz. (500 gr) beef cubes
1 lb. 2 oz. (500 gr) pork (lean shoulder)
1 lb. 2 oz. (500 gr) pork fat (non-smoked bacon)

To each pound of meat add:

⅓ teaspoon (1.5 gr) pepper
1 tablespoon (10 gr) salt
  pinch each of cinnamon, majoram, ginger and cardamon
  some potato puree
3 eggs
  garlic

Grind all meats well in meat grinder or food chopper. Mix well adding all spices. **Important:** Mix and knead with both hands into a smooth pate mixture (until bubbles form between fingers). Place into a greased loaf type pan and bake at 350°F. for 2 hours.

SAUERBRATEN
(Marinated Beef)

Joan Schoenleber

1 cup (237 ml) vinegar	1½ lbs. (680 gr) top round beef
1 teaspoon salt	2 tablespoons butter
5 peppercorns	¾ cup (178 ml) water
1 bay leaf	½ cup (118 ml) sour cream
1 chopped onion	

Combine marinade (first 5 ingredients) and bring to boil. When mixture cools, add raw meat. Refrigerate for several days. Drain, dry meat, set aside liquid. In heavy pot, melt butter, add meat, cook until well browned. add marinade and boiling water. Simmer until meat is tender. 10 minutes before serving, add sour cream.

SAUERBRATEN
(Marinated Pot Roast)

Claire Runge

Boil a mixture of half water, half vinegar. Pour this over the meat (eye of the round). If you prepare enough liquid to cover the meat, you won't have to turn the meat. It should marinate three days. Maybe during this time, even though the meat doesn't have to be turned, you might just "stir up" the marinade. After you have poured the water/vinegar over the meat, add salt, pepper, half onion cut up, tomato cut up, pot herbs, bay leaf (off hand, I would say add anything else you would like to). I use a pressure cooker and it does very well. After it is done, drain the liquid and make your gravy. For a "typical" Sauerbraten gravy you may want to add more vinegar.
Serve with 'Grüne Klösse', potato dumplings.

SAUERBRATEN
Leni Holzhauser

(Marinated Roast)

Rub a 5 to 6 pound (2 Kilo) piece of bottom round of beef with salt and pepper. Cut 1 garlic clove into thin slivers and with a sharp knife insert them into the meat. Put the meat into a large bowl and cover it with thin slices of onions. In a saucepan boil together 4 cups water (950 ml), $\frac{1}{3}$ cup (80 ml) wine vinegar, ½ lemon, (sliced and seeded) 6 peppercorns, 2 bay leaves, and 4 whole cloves. Pour the hot marinade over the meat and refrigerate it, covered tightly for 24 hours. Turn the beef several times as it marinates.

In a Dutch oven saute 2 onions, coarsely chopped in a ½ stick or ¼ cup (57 gr) butter. Remove the meat from the marinade, reserving 2 cups (474 ml) and dust it lightly with flour. Push the onions to the side of the pan, add the meat, and brown it on all sides. Add the reserved marinade with one carrot, finely chopped, 2 tablespoons tomato puree, 1 teaspoon sugar and a generous dash of paprika. Simmer the meat, covered, for about 3 hours or until it is tender. Remove it to a heated platter. Skim off all fat from the liquid and thicken the liquid, if desired with some gingersnaps or spice cookies.

SAUERBRATEN
Ruth Olivier

(Easy Marinated Roast)

1 chuck roast (or any other beef roast)	1 bottle of ketchup
2 large onions	mustard

Spread mustard thickly on all sides of the meat. Put into pot (with lid), add the diced onions, the whole bottle of ketchup, a little water so that the meat won't stick, cover and let simmer until meat is done. Add a little water from time to time, season to taste, and voila — Sauerbraten!

SAUERBRATEN
Alma M. DeMott

(Marinated Beef)

When my parents moved to Texas, mother used this as her company dinner there. I don't think anyone ever refused a dinner invitation for this!

3 lbs. (1 ⅓ Kilo) beef	12 cloves
cider vinegar	6 tablespoons shortening
water	¼ cup (50 gr) sugar
salt and pepper	6 gingersnaps
3 onion slices	½ cup (58 gr) flour
3 bay leaves	1 cup (237 ml) sour cream
1 teaspoon peppercorns	

Use top sirloin or bottom round of beef and have the butcher lard it. Wipe meat with a damp cloth and rub with salt and pepper. Place in a large bowl. Heat equal parts of water and vinegar to half cover the meat. Add sliced onions, bay leaves and peppercorns, cloves and sugar. When mixture is hot, pour over meat. Cover with a tight fitting lid and place in refrigerator 3 days in summer, 8 days in winter, turning every day. Remove and drain thoroughly (save vinegar). Heat the shortening in a heavy iron pan, add meat and brown well. Add vinegar and ginger snaps. Cover tightly and simmer 3 to 4 hours. When tender remove to a hot platter and add to the liquid in the pan the flour which has been mixed with the sour cream. Stir until thickened, strain and serve.

SAUERBRATEN FLEISCHKLÖSSE
(Sauerbraten Meatballs)   Helga Melton

Meatballs:

2 eggs	1 teaspoon freshly ground peppercorns
¾ cup (178 ml) milk	3 slices bread, broken into small pieces
1 tablespoon salt	4½ lbs. (2 Kilo) lean ground beef

Mix eggs, milk, seasonings together and pour over bread. Let stand for a few minutes and then work into paste. Combine with ground beef. Shape into patties, place on ungreased baking pan. Bake until brown in a 450° oven. Cool and then freeze or use in the sauce below.

Sauce:

4 slices bacon, cut into chunks
3 cups (711 ml) beef stock or water and instant beef flavor bouillon
4 tablespoons red wine vinegar
3 tablespoons brown sugar
1 onion, finely chopped
  salt to taste
1 cup gingersnap crumbs (about 16 large gingersnaps)

Fry bacon until crisp, sauté onions until golden and tender. Add stock, vinegar, sugar, salt and cook for 3 - 4 minutes. Add some of this sauce to gingersnaps to make a paste. Add paste to remaining sauce.

REISFRIKADELLEN
(Small Hamburgers with Rice)   Kris Jeter

A handwritten recipe found in my grandmother's 1912 cookbook.

1 cup (200 gr) leftover rice	½-¾ cup (120-180 ml) leftover meat
onion, chopped	½-¾ cup (120-180 ml) ground pork
1 tablespoon fat	½-¾ cup (120-180 ml) ground beef
1 egg	
parsley, salt, pepper, 1 tablespoon flour, sour cream, beefstock	

Brown the cooked rice with the onion in the fat. Mix with meat; add egg. Add parsley, season with salt and pepper. Shape into patties and brown on both sides. Make a gravy with the pan drippings, flour, stock and sour cream. Pour over the hamburgers when serving.

EINTOPF
(Pot Pie)

Marni Stauffer

Stew a chicken as you prefer. Remove chicken, remove meat to serve separately as desired.

Pot Pie Dough: Combine 3 cups (345 gr) flour, 3 teaspoons baking powder, a dash of salt and 3 well-beaten eggs and mix well. Add just enough milk to moisten. Roll out as you would for pie crust. Cut into large pieces, roughly 2'' by 3''. Place one at a time into boiling chicken liquid. Add some parsley flakes between layers. I like to put a layer of pot pie, then some sliced potatoes and thinly sliced onion and repeat layers. Liquid should be ample enough. Cover and boil for about 20 minutes. (The potatoes and onion are not always used.)

KANINCHENBRATEN
(Roasted Tame Rabbit)

Anneliese Chase

Tame rabbit is the most ideal diet meat, very low in fat but with a most delicate flavor, hovering between that of milk-fed veal and top chicken — yet more interesting.
My foster father (a baker in Berlin), raised his own rabbits in his Schrebergarten mostly for showing. Those which didn't make the grade, ended up being treats on our Sunday and holiday dinner table. Of course, the roasting was done in the big bakery oven and never again have I had such crispy yet tender and juicy rabbit. A few times I have been able to get a rabbit from a private breeder but one can usually get them fresh in the Italian market in Philadelphia.

Wash a skinned, cleaned, young rabbit and slighly salt it. Put into roasting pan chest down. Cover back and legs with bacon slices. Put into preheated 325° oven. After about 30 min. add ½ cup (118 ml) of chicken broth or water and skim off fat. Baste several times during the 1½ - 2 hour roasting time. Remove and discard bacon strips at least ½ hour before done. Cut into serving pieces, keep warm while thickening the pan juices with cornstarch and adding salt and pepper to taste (if you are not on a diet, add some sour cream).
Serve with red cabbage, boiled potatoes (Salzkartoffeln) or dumplings (Klösse).

HASENPFEFFER
(Rabbit Stew)

Leni Holzhauser

This dish is prepared exactly the same as Sauerbraten. Use the recipe for

Sauerbraten; prepare everything exactly as directed there, the only difference being that you use rabbit instead of the beef. It is soaked beforehand the same way and cooked the same way.

REHRÜCKEN
(Saddle of Venison)

Johanna Rosselli

4 oz. (100 gr) salt pork
2 lbs. (950 gr) saddle of venison (the whole saddle might be 4-5 lbs.) and it is advisable to roast the entire piece.)
salt, pepper, juniper berries   2 tablespoons flour
4 tablespoons (60 gr) butter   3 cups (⅞ liter) sour cream

Cut salt pork into long thin strips and with a larding needle or sharp thin knife insert into saddle about 1'' apart. Season saddle with salt and pepper and rub with crushed juniper berries. Heat butter in roasting pan, place roast, rounded side up, in the pan and roast for about 45 minutes, adding ¼ liter of boiling water and basting the roast frequently.

Before serving, cut the roast away from the bones with a sharp knife, slice it into thin slices, then reshape the saddle pushing the slices tightly together. With pan drippings make gravy, adding sour cream last.

JÄGERSCHNITZEL
(Hunter's Veal Cutlet)

Margarete G. Geyer

4 veal cutlets (6 oz. each)   1 cup (115 gr) flour
salt and pepper to taste   6 tablespoons (90 gr) butter
1 cup Pfefferlinge (pepper mushrooms), canned or dried. Sliced domestic mushrooms are also suitable. I use about 4-5 cups (950-1180 ml), however.
1 handful chopped parsley
1-2 onions, chopped (according to taste)
¾ cup cooked and diced bacon (about 6 slices)
1 cup (237 ml) heavy cream

Pound the veal with a mallet or the back of a cleaver until it is tender. Season with salt and pepper. Dredge in flour and sauté in the butter (two at a time if pan is big enough, one at a time if it isn't; if you do them one at a time, use less butter). Brown lightly, two or three minutes for each side. Remove the cutlets when done and keep them warm. Add the mushrooms, parsley, onions and bacon to the fat in the pan. Sauté just until warm. Stir in the cream. Arrange the meat on a serving platter or individual plates and pour the sauce over it.

SCHWARZSAUER
(Blacksour)

Walter Kruse's mother

This is similar to Hasenpfeffer, but with another kind of meat.

   1 lb. (454 gr) bacon, whole, then divided into 4 large chunks
3-4 pork kidneys, cut in half   4 cups (950 ml) blood from beef, strained
   1 pork heart, cut into quarters   4-5 bay leaves
     vinegar

Boil the pork pieces in a stock of bay leaves, vinegar and water, enough to cover all the pieces for about 30 minutes. Remove meat pieces. Over reduced heat add the blood slowly (only letting it drip into the stock!) Bring to a boil. Add meat again, bring to a boil, then reduce the heat and simmer until the sauce thickens and the meat is done. (About 2 hours) The sauce will be almost black. If it gets too thick, add a little more vinegar-water.
Serve with potatoes or dumplings.

SCHMORBRATEN
(Braised Pot Roast)

Johanna Rosselli

1-1½ lbs. (500-600 gr) boneless beef roast
   2 slices (40 gr) salt pork, cut into strips
     salt, pepper   1 bay leaf
   3 tablespoons (20 gr) flour   5 peppercorns
   3 tablespoons (40 gr) butter   1 piece of dark rind of rye bread
   1 medium onion, carrot,   3½ cups (⅞ liter) sour cream
     celery (soup greens)

If the meat is lean, it can be larded with the salt pork. Season roast with salt and pepper, turn in flour. Brown meat on all sides in the hot butter. Cut up the soup greens and add with the bread and sour cream to the pot. Add boiling water, enough to bring juice level half way up the roast. Cover pot and simmer the meat for 2 hours, turning it a few times. Strain the sauce through a sieve and pour over the sliced roast, when serving with potato or bread dumplings, sauerkraut or red cabbage.

SAFTGULASCH
(Goulash)

Helga Herglotz-Kissell

   2 lbs. (950 gr) beef cubes   ½ teaspoon each of salt,
   1 lb. (454 gr) onions   caraway seed, marjoram
   1 cup (227 gr) bacon fat (lard, shortening) 2 crushed garlic cloves
   1 tablespoon paprika   1 tablespoon tomato paste
   ¼ pint (112 ml) water   1 tablespoon flour to thicken

Sauté the finely chopped onions in the bacon fat until golden brown. Add the paprika and other spices, stirring well. Add the beef cubes and roast till browned, stirring frequently. Pour over the water and simmer constantly until the meat is tender and a thick gravy has formed.
This can be served over dumplings, boiled potatoes, rice or with crispy rolls.

KASSELER RIPPESPEER

(Pork Loin)

Ellen Stixrude

2-3 lbs. (900-1350) gr) pork loin roast, smoked
1 cup (237 ml) hot water   1 tomato
1 onion   4-5 tablespoons sour cream
1 teaspoon cornstarch, dissolved in 1 tablespoon cold water

Wash and dry the roast (do not salt). Cut the skin criss-cross. Put roast on the rack of the roasting pan, which has been rinsed with cold water. Roast at 350°. During the one hour roasting time, add hot water, the onion and the tomato. Make a gravy with the pan drippings, loosened from the sides of the pan with water, the sour cream and a little cornstarch. Season with salt and pepper.

ROULADEN

(Rolled stuffed steaks)

Ellen Stixrude

Use chipsteak - large whole slices
Salt and pepper each slice lightly; spread with a thin layer of horseradish mustard. Put a folded slice of bacon in the middle and top with 2 half slices of onion. Roll and secure with toothpicks or thread. Brown in margarine. Add hot water and 1 bayleaf. Cover and simmer for approximately 2 hours. Take out Rouladen and keep warm. Make gravy by adding as much hot water as necessary. Return meat to hot gravy and serve.

ROULADEN

(Braised Beef Rolls)

Trudy Rueggeberg

In a heavy iron skillet, with tight fitting lid, brown 4 or 5 quartered onions lightly, using bacon fat, suet or lard. Remove onions, set aside.
Cut bottom or top round (about ¼" thick) into 4" x 6 " pieces. Use wooden mallet to further flatten the pieces. Salt and pepper the meat, add a little mustard, place a thin slice of onion and raw bacon slices on the meat. Roll up each piece tightly and fasten with string or toothpick. Roll meat in flour. To the fat in the skillet add 8 peppercorns and 2 bayleaves, then add the meat, placing pieces close together and brown **very slowly**. When browned on one side, turn the meatrolls over and brown on the other (browning usually takes about 15 minutes, turn after 7). When both sides are browned, add browned onions and pour enough boiling water from the side, to half cover the meatrolls. Put the lid on tightly. Simmer about 40 minutes (no peeking allowed).
Remove meat from pot, and cut strings. Keep meatrolls warm, while making the gravy. To make the gravy, add water or flour as necessary to the liquid in the skillet to thicken (gravy may be strained). When gravy is finished, add the meatrolls and serve hot.

Suggestions: For 10 people (about 10 meatrolls) you need about 8 pounds of well trimmed round. You can get about 10 meatrolls to one layer. You may add another layer on top, but no more (second layer must be browned, of course, before adding).

RINDSROULADEN
(Rolled Stuffed Steaks)

Edith Dommert

4 slices of tender round steak, about ¼ inch thick
salt and freshly ground pepper   1 tablespoon bacon drippings
4 teaspoons prepared brown mustard 2-2½ cups (475 ml) water or bouillon
2 slices bacon, cut in half   1-2 teaspoons cornstarch
4 tablespoons finely chopped onions   1 tablespoon sour cream
4 pickles, cut in quarters   salt and pepper
4 small slices rye bread, cut in quarters   cotton thread

Lay the slices of beef flat on a surface and season with salt and pepper. Spread 1 teaspoon mustard over each slice, put 1 piece of bacon on the end of each slice of beef, along with 1 tablespoon chopped onions, 1 pickle, cut, 1 slice rye bread, cut. Roll the beef up tightly, making sure that it is well closed. Tie cotton thread around it to hold it securely. Heat bacon drippings in a heavy kettle or Dutch oven and add the beef rouladen. Saute on all sides until nicely brown. Add water or bouillon. Bring to a boil and simmer for about 2 hours. Remove beef rouladen and place on a preheated serving platter. Mix cornstarch and sour cream and add to the gravy. Stir continually and cook over moderate heat until boiling and cooked to desired thickness.
Pour some of the gravy over the rouladen, serve the rest of the gravy on the side.

SPÄTZLE
(Fresh Noodles)

Martha Borbe

3 cups (345 gr) flour   1 teaspoon salt
3 eggs   ¼ cup (60 ml) water
     (perhaps more water depending on dough)

Sift flour and salt into bowl. Add eggs and mix. Add water gradually until mixture is stiff but smooth. Press dough on a floured board. With a sharp knife scrape small pieces of dough off and drop into boiling salted water. Boil gently 5 - 8 min. until they come to top of water. Remove from water with perforated spoon and drain in cold water. Serve with sauce.

SPÄTZLE
(Fresh Noodles)

Ingrid Torres

4 cups (460 gr) flour   2 eggs
1 teaspoon salt   1 cup (237 ml) water

Sift the flour and salt into a bowl and make a well in the center. Add the eggs and mix together. Stir in the water gradually, beating well after each addition.

Beat the mixture till batter shows air bubbles.

Dip a pastry board in cold water. Spread a spoonful of dough on it and then hold the board at a slant over a pan of lightly salted boiling water. Using a spatula, scrape thin strips, about ¼" wide, into the water, When the noodles rise to the surface, remove with a perforated spoon. Rinse in hot or cold water. Drain the Spätzle in a sieve and keep warm in a covered dish until all the dough has been used.

Serves 4-6.

SPÄTZLE
(Fresh Noodles)

Elsie Roser-Lister

My father enjoyed these noodles, a recipe from his hometown, Besigheim.

1½ cups (260 gr) flour	2 eggs
¼ teaspoon salt	1 cup (237 ml) water

Mix ingredients together until mixture is smooth. Press dough on a floured board or use a Spätzle machine. Cut small pieces of dough off and drop into boiling water. Cook approximately 2 minutes or until noodles rise to top of water. Remove from water with slotted spoon and drain in cold water.

SERVIETTENKNÖDEL
(Napkin Dumplings)

Margit G. Herglotz

This dumpling goes very well with the Saftgulasch.

9 medium sized rolls	2 eggs
4 tablespoons (57 gr) shortening	some flour
2 cups (474 ml) milk	some salt

Cut 6 rolls in small cubes and brown lightly in the shortening. Cut the other 3 rolls in slices and soak them in 1 cup of the milk until soaked through. Mix the other cup of milk with the 2 eggs, the flour, and the salt until you have a thin well dripping dough. Pour this dough over the well soaked slices of rolls, stirring all the ingredients into a loose dough consistency. To this add the browned bread cubes. Drop this mass into a moist, cold wrung-out cotton cloth, shaping the dough into a long loaf and hang into pot filled with boiling salt water for 1 hour. Boiling must never stop until done. After 1 hour, carefully remove dumpling and slice into thin slices with a sewing thread.

This is a side dish that can be served with meats, salads, gravies, stewed fruits, etc.

SEMMELKLÖSSE
(Bread Dumplings)

Johanna Rosselli

8 leftover rolls	parsley
salt	marjoram
1 small onion, chopped	1½ cups (⅜ liter) milk
3 tablespoons (40 gr) butter	2 eggs

Slice rolls into thin slices. Sauté onions in the butter, add chopped parsley and marjoram. Pour over rolls. Stir eggs and milk and add to the rolls. Mix everything well into firm dough. Form into balls with wet hands, and drop gently into lightly salted boiling water. Let simmer for 20 minutes, uncovered.

Serve with 'Schmorbraten', something sour or 'Silesian Heaven', something sweet!

KARTOFFELKLÖSSE
(Potato Dumplings)

Johanna Rosselli

2 lbs. (950 gr) or 6-8 medium boiled potatoes, baking variety
2 cups (250 gr) flour or 1 cup + 2 tablespoons (200 gr) farina

1 egg	croutons
salt	butter

Peel and grate or rice the boiled potatoes. Mix with flour or farina, egg and salt and knead into dough which should not stick, otherwise add more flour. Make a trial dumpling; roll it in flour. Drop gently into boiling water and simmer uncovered for 15 minutes. If it falls apart, add more flour or farina to the dough. Make long, 4-5 cm. thick rolls, cut off piece by piece and form dumplings, putting a few roasted croutons in the middle. Roll dumplings in flour and drop into the boiling salted water. Simmer for 15 minutes, uncovered. Good luck!

KARTOFFELKLÖSSE
((Potato Dumplings)

Leni Holzhauser

5 medium potatoes	2 eggs
1½ cups (225 gr) bread crumbs	1 tablespoon flour
2 teaspoons grated onions	salt and pepper

Grate 5 medium raw potatoes, press out as much moisture as possible, and add 1½ cups bread crumbs and 2 teaspoons grated onions. Stir in 2 eggs, beaten, 1 tablespoon flour and salt and pepper to taste. With floured fingers shape the mixture into balls the size of a large walnut and dust them lightly with flour. Drop the dumplings into boiling salted water and boil them, covered tightly for 15 minutes. Remove them from the water with a slotted spoon.

BACKOBST UND KLÖSSE
(Dried Fruit and Dumplings)

Ellen Stixrude

Dried fruit includes prunes, apples, apricots or pears. Make favorite fruit compote recipe with dried fruits, a little water and lemon peel, thickened with a little cornstarch.

Dumplings:

2 cups (½ liter) milk
½ cup (113 gr) butter
1 teaspoon salt

1-2 eggs (1 large or 2 small)
1½-2 cups (175-230 gr) flour

Bring milk, butter and salt to a boil. Remove from flame. Gradually add flour; beat well until smooth and dry. Add eggs. Form small dumplings with a spoon and drop into lightly salted boiling water. Simmer until dumplings rise to the top. (Dip spoon into boiling water between forming the dumplings.)

To serve, spoon fruit compote over dumplings.

SCHLESISCHES HIMMELREICH
(Silesian Heaven)

Johanna Rosselli

Often sung about, always cooked and loved the most, this is the Silesian's national dish: his heaven on earth!

9 oz. (250 gr) mixed dried fruit
1 lb. 2 oz. (500 gr) pork or corned beef
    salt

4 tablespoons (50 gr) butter
¼ cup (30 gr) flour
sugar
a little lemon juice

Soak the dried fruit mixture overnight in ½ liter water. Cook pork in 1 liter hot water without salt for about one hour. If using corned beef, start the beef in cold water, then simmer for one hour. Add the fruit mixture and simmer until the meat is soft. Make a roux from the butter and flour; add the sauce. Season with salt and sugar and a few drops of lemon juice. Pour over the sliced meat. Serve with bread dumplings.

MEHLBEUTEL
(Dumpling)

4 cups (1 lb. or 454 gr) flour
2 cups (474 ml) milk
5-6 eggs

pinch salt
¾ cup (125 gr) raisins

In a large bowl mix flour with the egg yolks, using a wooden spoon. Add enough milk to make a smooth dough that will fall (or drop) off the spoon. Add salt. Beat egg whites stiff and fold into dough.

Put a 20 inch square of linen (linen napkin) into a bowl and moisten it lightly with water. Dust with flour. Put the washed and dried raisins on the square cloth, pour the batter over it. Gather the cloth on the top and tie it firmly with a strong cotton thread. The dough will expand while cooking, so leave enough space above the dough. Fill a big enough pot half full with water; bring water to a boil. Put a saucer in the bottom of the pot to keep the dumpling away from the bottom or suspend the napkin from a long spoon into the water without touching the bottom of the pot. Keep the water simmering; if necessary add more **hot** water to keep the dumpling covered. (Cold water will deflate the dumpling.) Allow about 1½ to 2 hours cooking time. Serve with melted butter and sugar, dried fruit stew or rhubarb or gooseberry sauce. Variations: Instead of raisins, pitted sour cherries can be used. These are added to the batter at the end, before putting it on the napkin.

ORIGINAL DITHMARSCHER MEHLBEUTEL
(The Original Dithmarsch Dumpling)
A north German speciality.

Walter Kruse's mother

4 cups (1 lb. or 454 gr) flour
2 cups (474 ml) milk
5-6 eggs

salt
1 pork jowl
boiling potatoes (boiled in the skin)

Prepare the pork jowl, boiling it in water for ½ hour. Add the dumpling by putting the linen bag either on the saucer or suspending it from a spoon (as prepared in the previous recipe.) Simmer for ½ hour. Add potatoes in the skin and simmer ½ hour longer.
Serve first: the dumpling with butter and sugar
Serve next: the pork jowl and potatoes with mustard (potatoes are peeled after boiling.)

SCHWARZER MEHLBEUTEL
(Black Flour Dumpling)

Walter Kruse's mother

4 cups (1 lb. or 454 gr) flour
½ cup (118 ml) blood from beef
½ cup (118 ml) milk
½ cup (113 gr) pork fat,
   rendered - saltpork
   saltpork fat pieces, optional

½ cup (80 gr) raisins
1 cup (237 ml) finely diced apples
1 cup (237 gr) grated raw or cooked
   potato
pinch salt
pinch ground cloves

In a large bowl mix milk, strained blood and flour with a wooden spoon. Add the hot dripping pork fat, the grated potatoes, apples and raisins and spices and work into a heavy batter. Proceed by following directions for Mehlbeutel (flour dumplings) recipe. Cook about 2 - 2½ hours. Serve with diced sauteed pork fat and syrup.

SAUERKRAUT UND SCHWEINEFLEISCH
Anna Herold
(Pork with Sauerkraut)

2 tablespoons shortening	2 tablespoons paprika
1 cup (85 gr) chopped onions	1½-2 cups (350-475 ml) boiling water
2 lbs. (950 gr) pork shoulder cut in cubes	1 large can (or as desired) sauerkraut
½ teaspoon salt, a little pepper	1 cup (237 ml) sour cream

Heat shortening in-dutch oven. Sauté onion until transparent. Add pork and sauté together for about 10 min. Add salt, pepper and paprika. Stir well. Add enough water to cover meat. Drain sauerkraut, arrange over meat. Cover, simmer until meat is tender about 1½ hours. Fold in sour cream and stir to blend. Bring to boiling point (but do not boil), stir to blend flavors.

Serves 4-6 people.

SAUERKRAUT MIT EISBEIN
Ruth Bischoff
(Sauerkraut with Pork Hocks)

¾ lb. (340 gr) pork hocks	1 raw potato
water to cover	salt and sugar mixture
¾ lb. (340 gr) sauerkraut	

Place meat covered in pot of water, bring to boil, then simmer for 1½ hours. Add sauerkraut to the hocks and juice and continue to simmer for 1½ hours. Add a grated raw potato as a thickener to the sauerkraut. Season with salt, pepper and sugar. Serve with mashed potatoes and pea puree.

STECKRÜBEN-EINTOPF
Annemarie Rawe
(Turnip Stew)

1 lb. (454 gr) cubed pork	1 lb. (454 gr) potatoes, washed, peeled, diced
3-4 onions, chopped	
1 medium turnip, washed and peeled, diced	salt and pepper
2 cups (474 ml) beef broth	3 tablespoons oil or margarine

Fry meat with onions in fat; do not brown too much. Season with salt and pepper; add turnips and sauté lightly. Add beef stock and potatoes; simmer over low heat until the stew thickens slightly. Add freshly ground pepper before serving.

GURKEN MIT FLEISCHFÜLLUNG
(Stuffed Cucumbers)   Brigitte Conrad

1 lb. (454 gr) ground meat	1 medium onion, minced
4 green cucumbers	salt and pepper to taste
1 egg	½-¾ cups (75-115 gr) bread crumbs

Peel the cucumbers, cut lengthwise in halves, scoop out soft inner parts. Put aside for later use. Prepare the ground meat mixing it with one whole egg, minced onions, bread crumbs and salt and pepper to taste. Mince some bacon (or ham ends) and onion for frying. Stuff the cucumber halves with the meat and tie the two halves together with a thread. Fry bacon and onion and the 4 cucumbers on both sides to a light brown. Put in the soft scooped out parts which had been set aside, add water and bouillon cubes or broth to fill half the pan. Cover pan and cook for 15 - 20 minutes until cucumbers are soft. Lift out and thicken broth to make a light gravy.
Serve with potatoes sprinkled with fresh parsley.

BRATKARTOFFELN
(Home Fries)   Bernd Lippe

cooked potatoes, sliced	diced onion, to taste
butter, to taste	soy sauce (a few spritzers)
salt and pepper, to taste	marjoram, caraway seeds, to taste

Melt butter in skillet. Add sliced potatoes and dash of each spice and fry until light brown.
Try it, you'll like it!

GEFÜLLTES METERBROT
(Sausage Loaf)   Hilde Cox

1 loaf French bread	3 tablespoons minced parsley
1 lb. (454 gr) sausage	1 tablespoon minced shallots
½ cup (75 gr) bread crumbs	1 slightly beaten egg
½ cup (56 gr) grated cheddar cheese	salt, pepper
6 medium mushrooms	

Cut away bottom crust of French bread, scoop out soft part, make bread crumbs with it. Fry sausage without casing, degrease, put for a few seconds in blender to get fine consistency. Sauté mushrooms (chopped finely) and shallots in pan drippings. Mix everything (save some cheddar to sprinkle over loaf) and fill French loaf. Bake at 350° for about 20 minutes.
Can be made ahead and frozen.

ANGEMACHTER CAMEMBERT　Hilde Cox
(Camembert Spread)

1 4-oz. Camembert	2 tablespoons white wine
2 tablespoons butter	salt, pepper, paprika
½ tablespoon onion	

With fork mix Camembert and butter until well blended. Add wine and mix. Add finely minced onion or shallot, season with salt and pepper, sprinkle paprika over the cheese mixture. Serve with crackers or spread on slices of rye bread.
Serve with a dry white wine, Franconian or Pfälzer.

HAUSGEMACHTE BRATWURST　Hilde Cox

I spent a lot of time trying to duplicate the pork sausages my hometown is famous for. The sausage made in Denver, PA comes closest. It has to be gray and crumbly in texture. This is the recipe I got from a butcher in Neustadt:

3 lbs. (1350 gr) ground pork from shoulder or rib end

3 teaspoons salt	1 teaspoon marjoram
1 teaspoon pepper	½ teaspoon allspice

Grind pork in coarse food mill, mix spices and knead everything by hand until well blended (use hands for best results). Fill in casings or make patties. Fry and serve with mustard, horseradish and rye bread, or even sauerkraut. The kraut is warmed up in the degreased pan drippings.

GROSSER HANS　Renate Muendel
(Steamed Pudding)

Cream 1 cup (2 sticks or 227 gr) margarine with ½ cup (100 gr) sugar and 5 egg yolks. Add juice and grated rind of 1 lemon, 6 cups (700 gr) flour, 2 tablespoons baking powder, ¼ cup (45 gr) raisins, ¼ cup (35 gr) chopped nuts or almonds, a little milk, and 5 stiffly beaten egg whites.
Pour into a greased and breaded Savarin form (about ¾ full), close its lid and set into a big pot of boiling water. Water should come up to ¾ height of form. Steam it for 1¾ hours; then open the form and let the pudding get crisp and light brown in a 350° oven for 15 minutes. Cool slightly, loosen in the form and invert. Serve with fruit (stewed rhubarb or plums) or wine sauce.

Wine Sauce:

Heat, without boiling, in top of double boiler: 2 eggs, 1 cup (¼ liter) wine, 1 cup (¼ liter) water, 2 heaping teaspoons cornstarch, 1 lemon (juice and grated rind), sugar to taste. Heat till thickened and serve warm.

Afternoon KAFFEETRINKEN

Ellen Stixrude

We always observe this custom in the afternoon with cookies, cake or pastry. The first question the children ask when they come home from school is: "What's for coffee?" They, however, only drink hot chocolate or tea!

TAUSEND-JAHRS-KUCHEN

Renate Muendel

(1,000 Years Cookies)

As the name indicates, they keep forever!

Cream 1 cup (227 gr) butter and 2 cups (400 gr) sugar,
    4 cups (460 gr) flour,
    6 eggs
       the rind of 1-1½ lemons
       a dash of vanilla
    ½ lb. (230 gr) blanched ground almonds.

Drop on greased cookie sheet by the teaspoon. Bake till light golden at 375°F.

Makes about 5 dozen cookies.

AMERIKANER

Elly Gilgenast

(Old Fashioned German Vanilla Cookies)

2 cups (230 gr) sifted flour	7 tablespoons (100 gr) butter
3 teaspoons baking powder	½ cup (100 gr) sugar
1-3 oz. package instant	2 large eggs
vanilla pudding	1 teaspoon vanilla
6 tablespoons milk	

Frosting: 2 cups (260 gr) powdered sugar, sifted
         1 tablespoon cocoa

Sift the flour again together with the baking powder and set aside. Mix the vanilla pudding with the milk and set aside. Cream the butter and slowly add the sugar, eggs (one at a time), vanilla, and the pudding mixture. Then add the flour mixture, a tablespoon at a time until well blended. Drop rounded tablespoonfuls of dough 2 inches apart onto a lightly greased cookie sheet and bake in a preheated oven at 325° for 13 - 15 minutes. The cookies are done when no indention remains when the cookie is touched lightly. For the frosting, mix the powdered sugar with enough hot water to make an easily spreadable frosting. Cover the underside of half of the cookies with half of the frosting. Into the remaining mixture stir the cocoa and cover the underside of the remaining cookies. (Each cookie is half vanilla and half chocolate frosting!)
Makes about 2 dozen.

IGEL
Kris Jeter
(Hedge Hog)

Included in my grandmother's 1912 handwritten cookbook.

Melt ½ lb. (227 gr) semisweet chocolate; add 1 cup (227 gr) crisco or other shortening and 2 eggs. Mix well and cook until thickened. Put lady fingers on a cake plate shaping them into the form of a hedge hog; alternating with layers of the chocolate frosting. End with frosting and decorate with blanched, slivered almonds to look like a hedge hog.

HOBELSPÄNE ODER RÄDERKUCHEN
(Wood Shavings or Wheel Cakes)
Erica Stoyer

4 cups (500 gr) flour	3 eggs
1 teaspoon baking powder	4 tablespoons milk or water
½ cup (100 gr) sugar	10 tablespoons (125 gr) butter
4 drops of Dr. Oetker Lemon extract	oil or lard or Crisco for deep frying
1 little bottle of	
Dr. Oetker rum flavoring	

Sift flour with baking powder onto table or baking board. Make well in the middle. Put sugar, lemon, rum flavoring, eggs and milk into the well. Mix everything and work into a thick batter with some of the flour. Cut cold butter on top of the batter, cover with some of the flour, then knead everything quickly into a smooth dough. Roll out dough to ¼" thickness. Cut long strips using a fluted wheel. Cut a slit into the middle of each strip, pull the end of a strip through the slit to get the curl of wood shavings. Fry in hot oil or lard until brown. Lift out with a slotted spoon, dust with powdered sugar.

KALTER HUND-DIE ECHTE PALMIN-KEKSTORTE
Helga Walters
('Cold Dog' or Cookie Torte)

1 cup + 2 tablespoons (250 gr) Crisco	
2 eggs	1 teaspoon instant coffee
1¼ cup (250 gr) sugar	1 pinch of salt
½ cup (50-75 gr) cocoa	1 teaspoon rum
25 cookies (Bahlsen Tortenkekse) - available in international specialty shops	

Melt Crisco slowly. Beat eggs and sugar till light and lemon colored; add cocoa, salt, coffee, rum slowly. Little by little add liquified, cooled down Crisco. Take a small loaf pan and lay out with wax paper. Fill pan with a layer of cookies, then chocolate, then cookies, etc. ending with a layer of chocolate. Enjoy!

(This will freeze very well. Thaw out in refrigerator. Use twice the amount for a regular bread baking form.

APFELKUCHEN

Edith Dommert

100-125 g Butter oder Margarine
125 g Zucker
2-3 Eier
Salz, geriebene Zitrone,
Vanillin-Zucker
200 g Weizenmehl

2 gestrichene Teelöffel Backpulver
1-4 Esslöffel Milch
Butter oder Margarine
zum Einfetten der Springform
500-750 g Apfel
Puderzucker, Schlagsahne

Für den Teig Butter oder Margarine schaumig rühren, nach und nach Zucker, Eier, Salz, geriebene Zitrone, und Vanillin-Zucker hinzugeben. Weizenmehl und Backpulver mischen, sieben, und abwechselnd mit Milch unterrühren (nur so viel Milch verwenden, dass der Teig schwer reissend vom Löffel fällt).

Den Teig in eine mit Fett gefettete Springform füllen (Rand nicht fetten, Durchmesser etwa 26 cm) glattstreichen. Für den Belag die Äpfel schälen, vierteln, entkernen, mehrmals der Länge nach einritzen, kranzförmig auf den Teig legen. Backzeit 40-50 Minuten, 175-200° Celsius. Den erkalteten Kuchen mit Puderzucker bestäuben. Mit Schlagsahne servieren.

APFELKUCHEN
(Apple Cake)

½-⅔ cups (100-125 gr) butter or margarine
⅔ cup (125 gr) sugar
2-3 eggs
salt
grated lemon rind
9 gr vanilla sugar (from import shop) or ½ teaspoon vanilla extract
1¾ cups (200 gr) flour
2 level teaspoons baking powder
1-4 tablespoons milk
butter or margarine to grease springform base (not sides)
1-1½ lbs. (500-750 gr) apples
confectionery sugar
whipped cream

Cream butter or margarine until fluffy. Gradually add sugar, eggs, salt, grated lemon rind and vanilla sugar. Mix and sift flour and baking powder together and add alternately with milk to the butter mixture (use only as much milk as necessary so that dough sticks and peels slightly from spoon). Pour batter into a greased springform (diameter about 10 in). Smooth across. Peel, quarter and core apples. Then slash each quarter 6 - 8 times lengthwise in a fan shape, however, do not cut through the underside. Place apples in a circular form around and on the batter. Bake 40-50 minutes at 350-375°. Dust cake when cool with powdered sugar; serve with whipped cream.

APFELKUCHEN
(Apple Cake)

Trudy Gilgenast

Other fruit such as peaches or purple plums may also be used. This cake was often a summertime favorite in our family and one that my mother baked for our sweet tooth as well as for guests.

2 cups (230 gr) flour	2 teaspoons baking powder
½ cup (¼ lb. or 113 gr) butter	½ cup (100 gr) sugar
2 eggs	3-4 cups (700-950 ml) sliced apples

Mix sugar and butter, add eggs and then flour mixture. Spread on sheet pan (11½ by 17½ inches with an edge all around). Place sliced apples on top of dough in an overlapping fashion. Sprinkle crumbs on top of apples.

Crumbs:
½ stick (57 gr) butter
½ cup (58 gr) flour
½ cup (100 gr) sugar

Mix together with hands and spread over apples (or other fruit). Bake at 350°F for 45 minutes. Serve plain or with whipped cream.

Guten Appetit!

STREUSEL
(Another topping for Gilgenast-Applecake)

Elisabeth Kottenhahn

Brown breadcrumbs from dark or white bread with a little sugar, cinnamon and dash of red wine. Sprinkle over apples and dot with butter. Smells good; tastes delicious.

APFELKUCHEN
(Apple Cake)

Heli Fink

½ cup (113 gr) butter	grated rind of one lemon
1 cup (115 gr) flour	5-6 large green apples
⅓ cup (66 gr) sugar	¾ cup (178 ml) currant jelly
1 egg yolk	almonds, cinnamon
1 drop of vanilla extract	

Cream butter, sugar, egg and flour, lemon rind and vanilla, until batter is smooth. Pat with hand into a 9-10 inch springform. Dice apples and mix with the currant jelly. Spread over batter, sprinkle with cinnamon and almonds. Bake in 400° oven for one hour.

FEINE APFELSCHNITTEN
Jane Francis
(Apple Cake)

4 cups (500 gr) cake flour	¼ teaspoon salt
1 teaspoon baking powder	grated rind of 1 lemon
1-1¼ cups (250-300 gr) butter	4 lbs. (1.8 kilo) apples
½-⅔cups (100-125 gr) sugar	¾ cup (125 gr) raisins
2 eggs	

1 package vanilla sugar (available in gourmet shops) or 1 teaspoon vanilla
lemon or rum glaze made from 2 cups (250 gr) confectioner's sugar and
slightly diluted fresh lemon juice to make a thick glaze.

Sift together onto a board the flour, baking powder and salt. Make a well
in the center, add the eggs, stir them slightly working in a bit of the flour;
pour the sugar, then the lemon rind over everything. Cut the butter into the
dry ingredients with a pastry blender or two knives until the mixture is
the consistency of coarse corn meal. Knead the dough gently and quickly,
adding a bit more flour, into a smooth ball that no longer sticks.
Refrigerate dough for ½ hour. Roll out half of the dough on a floured
board and spread on a lightly greased pan 10 x 14 x 1. Peel, core and cut up
apples in thin slices, heap on dough in a layer 3-4 cm. thick leaving the edges
free. Scatter vanilla sugar and raisins over the apples. Roll out rest of dough
into a slightly smaller cover and spread it over the apples. For easier
handling, roll onto rolling pin and carefully unroll over pan. Prick cover
several times with a fork. Press around edges. Bake on center rack about
60 minutes in 350° oven. Glaze the cake while still hot. When slightly cooled,
cut into small squares and carefully lift from pan onto rack to cool completely.

APFELKUCHEN
Dorothy Kaeks
(Apple Cake)

Cake:

1 yeast cake (dissolve in ¼ cup (60 ml) warm water

2¾ cups (320 gr) all purpose flour	2 eggs
1 teaspoon salt	1 cup (200 gr) sugar
¼ lb. (113 gr) butter	2-3 teaspoons cinnamon
½ cup (118 ml) sour cream	1 tablespoon breadcrumbs (or cookie crumbs)

Apple Filling:

Drain 1 can (1 lb. 4 oz.) presliced apples on absorbent paper or use fresh
apples. Just before placing on dough, combine apples with:

½ cup (100 gr) sugar	1 teaspoon lemon rind
2 teaspoons cinnamon	¼ teaspoon nutmeg

Mix together carefully and spread on cake dough.

Dissolve yeast in ¼ cup warm water. Set aside. Mix flour and salt. Cut butter (one stick or ¼ lb) into flour until particles are fine. Add sour cream, 2 un-beaten eggs and the softened yeast. Mix together to form dough. Chill at least 2 hours. Combine sugar and cinnamon. Roll out ½ of dough mixture on a floured surface to the shape of a 15 x 8 inch rectangle. Sprinkle with 2 tablespoons of the sugar-cinnamon mixture, fold over dough in half and roll out again. Repeat this three times until sugar-cinnamon mixture is used up in the rolled out dough. Sprinkle breadcrumbs down center of dough, place half of filling over that, dot with butter. Fold one side of dough over filling, fold second side over, overlap and seal edges. Place seam side up on greased cookie sheet and make a circle out of cake joining each end. Make 4-5 slashes about 3 inches apart on top of cake. (I use a scissor to cut these). Let rise in a warm place about 1 hour. Bake at 350° for 35 minutes.

Dough is enough for 2 cakes. "Guten Appetit"

APFELKUCHEN
(Apple Cake)

Marie Holzhauser Martens

This recipe is one that I have Americanized. My mother always made a yeast cake; however, I prefer the following cake recipe. The topping, the same that my mother used, made this a favorite cake in our family as well as for our guests. Mother always had the Zion Lutheran church Frauenverein (Ladies Circle) at our home for their June meeting. The women looked forward to Mom's special cake with whipped cream!

Cake:
1 cup (115 gr) flour	1 egg
2 teaspoons cream of tartar	½ teaspoon vanilla
¼ teaspoon salt	2 tablespoons milk
2 tablespoons sugar	½ cup (85 gr) raisins
2 cups (475 ml) apples (sliced)	1 teaspoon cinnamon
1½ tablespoons butter	

Topping:
1 egg
½ cup (118 ml) milk
2 tablespoons sugar

Sift 1 cup flour. Resift with 2 teaspoons cream of tartar, ¼ teaspoon salt and 2 tablespoons sugar. Add 1½ tablespoon butter and work these ingredients like a pastry. Beat in 1 egg, ½ teaspoon vanilla and milk to make a stiff dough. Spread it with a lightly floured palm in a round or square greased 9 or 10 inch oven proof dish. Sprinkle raisins over top and then cover the top closely with apples. Sprinkle cinnamon over and dot with butter.

Topping:
Beat one egg with ½ cup milk and 2 tablespoons sugar and pour over top. Bake in a hot oven 425° for 25 minutes.

APFELKUCHEN MIT STREUSELN
(Apple Cake with Crumb Topping)   Erica Stoyer

½ cup (100 gr) butter
½ cup (100 gr) sugar
1 package vanillin sugar
   (available in gourmet shops)
   or 1 teaspoon vanilla
2 eggs
   pinch of salt

4 drops of Dr. Oetker lemon extract
1¼ cups (150 gr) flour
⅓ cup (50 gr) cornstarch
2 teaspoons baking powder
4 tablespoons milk
1 lb. (500 gr) apples

Topping:
1 cup (100 gr) flour
⅓ cup (75 gr) sugar

1 package vanillin sugar
5 tablespoons (75 gr) butter

Cream butter and sugar. Add vanillin sugar, eggs, salt and lemon. Sift flour with cornstarch and baking powder. Add alternately with the milk to the batter. The dough has the right consistency when it drops heavily from the spoon. Fill the dough into a greased 10 inch springform. Smooth it evenly with the back of a spoon frequently dipped into cold water. Peel and slice apples. Arrange the slices slightly overlapping in a wreath pattern, starting ¼ inch from the rim of the pan. For the streusel topping sift flour into a bowl, mix with sugar and vanillin sugar. Cut the cold butter into it and mix quickly with fingers or forks. Sprinkle over apples. Bake at 350° for 40 minutes. Dust with powdered sugar after baking or just before serving.

APFELSTRUDEL
(Apple Strudel)   Annelies B. Menta

We were four children at home. When one of us came home with good grades during the autumn, my mother made an Apfelstrudel as reward. Since we enjoyed this dish very much, we took turns in achieving high marks so we could eat our favorite meal as often as possible.

Dough:
2½ cups (290 gr) flour, sifted
1 egg
1 tablespoon oil

½ teaspoon salt
1 teaspoon lemon juice
½ cup (118 ml) warm water or less

Filling:
4 lbs. (1.8 kilo) apples
2 oz. rum
1 teaspoon cinnamon
1½ teaspoons vanillin sugar
   (available in gourmet shops
   or 1 teaspoon vanilla)

lemon rind
4 oz. (112 gr) currants
3 oz. (85 gr) melted butter
1 cup (150 gr) bread crumbs
½ cup (60 gr) ground almonds

Put all ingredients for dough into bowl and mix thoroughly. On floured board stretch and fold dough until elastic. Form dough into ball and let rest under inverted bowl for 30 minutes. In the meantime, prepare filling. Peel apples and cut into thin slices, add rum, cinnamon, vanillin sugar, lemon rind, and currants. Roll out dough with rolling pin as thinly as possible then stretch with hands until paper thin, final size should be about 16″ x 20″. Brush with melted butter, sprinkle with bread crumbs and almonds. Add apple filling and roll from long side to form roll. Place on greased baking sheet in crescent shape. Close ends tightly so no liquid can escape during baking. Brush with melted butter and bake for 30 minutes at 400°F. Dust with confectioner's sugar and serve with vanilla sauce.

APFELSCHEIBEN IN EIERTEIG Fannie Kummer
(Dessert Apple Fritters)

These are the best fritters I've tasted. Grandma always made them for my father, her only son-in-law.

Alma M. DeMott

½ cup (60 gr) flour	¾ cup (178 ml) milk
2 teaspoons baking powder	½ cup (100 gr) sugar
1 egg beaten lightly	¼ teaspoon salt
4 apples	flavor with vanilla

Pare and core apples and cut into circles ¼ inch thick. Sift together flour, baking powder, sugar and salt, two or three times. Add milk, eggs and flavoring. Dip each slice into batter and fry in deep hot fat, the same as crullers. Sprinkle with powdered sugar. Bananas or pineapple may be used the same way.

SANKT MARTINSTAG
(Saint Martin's and
November Memorial Days)

"Ich geh' mit meiner Laterne" — rings through the streets of villages, towns and cities as children sing and carry homemade lanterns bearing a lighted candle. Saint Martin's Day, November 11, is celebrated throughout Germany as a festival for children. Elementary-aged school children create a variety of designs and shapes which are cut out, covered with brightly colored transparent paper, formed into a lantern on the end of a long pole. On November 10, the eve of St. Martin's, groups of children march around the community and sing. Often they receive fruits, candies and nuts.

This is a very special day for young and old. A song tells of the Roman soldier, St. Martin, who befriended a beggar asking for alms on a cold day. Since he had nothing other than his warm cloak to share, he cut it in half with his sword and gave half to the beggar. According to legend St. Martin received a sign in a dream the next night in which Christ said that Martinus who was not yet baptized had protected him from the cold. In the year 372 A.D. Martin became Bishop of Tours under Roman rule and was celebrated for his humility and piety.

St. Martin's Day marks the beginning of the dark and cheerless period from autumn to winter. November is also known as the gray month due to the dreary fog-rain type weather and to the numerous religious days that seem to provoke sadness. St. Martin's Day is a light amongst these days and its celebration has literally involved light and fire. More recent processions involving children also focus on a white horse and a mounted figure representing St. Martin as a Roman soldier. In various market squares throughout West Germany scenes of the Martin-beggar episode take place. In some Protestant areas the celebration is said to honor Martin Luther, for after the Reformation Lutherans abolished the veneration of saints. It was just by chance that Luther's birthday was November 10 and protestant children were able to continue this lantern celebration. In some regions the emphasis is put on a more secular reference, on the light from the moon and stars.

Another custom attributed to this date was one involving domestic servants. It was on this day that jobs were changed or an existing agreement was extended depending upon the performance of the individual. Since this has an effect especially on herdsmen, cattle were put into their stalls on St. Martin's Day until the spring when the personnel was used again to take the animals out into the pasture.

The goose fattening period ended at this time of the year also and the farmer would sell off extra geese. In earlier times parsons demanded geese as payment for taxes due and gradually a custom developed to eat a goose on St. Martin's Day. Since this was also the time for slaughtering the first pigs, there was much eating, drinking and celebrating, which contributed, in part, to the harvest festival activities and parallel our Thanksgiving feast.

In general, November is a time for reflection and contemplation. The approach of winter and death in nature is also reflected in the holidays commemorating departed loved ones. 'Reformationstag' (Reformation Day) on October 31 is the commemoration of the Protestant Church breaking with the Roman doctrine in 1517.

'Allerheiligen' (All Saints Day) on November 1 is a memorial day in the Catholic church, set aside to honor all saints not accorded a special day. It is followed on November 2 by 'Allerseelen' (All Souls Day) which is dedicated to the memory of the dead. Visits to cemeteries and the placing of lighted candles and winter-type decorations on graves mark the special honor to departed souls.

'Totensonntag' (Sunday for the Dead) is celebrated by the Protestants on the last Sunday before the first Advent as a tribute to their dead. 'Buss- und Bettag' (Repentance Day), is on the Wednesday before the Sunday honoring the dead in the Protestant Church. Members are asked to reflect, reconsider their conduct and orient it to the moral laws of the Christian church. The serenity of this holiday, which is legal in all states except Bavaria, is noted in the absence of the playing of dance-type music.

November days pass quickly and are perhaps not as somber for the local German-Americans as for Germans in the homeland. This is also the month of bazaars sponsored by numerous organizations including local churches and ethnic groups. The women of these organizations work industriously throughout the year to prepare articles for sale. The ladies of the German-American Club enjoy working together as they fashion unique craft-type items or other 'Handarbeit' projects. During these activity sessions 'Kaffee und Kuchen', the most popular afternoon treat, is served. At the bazaar itself a Konditor's array of home-baked speciality cakes and cream-covered tortes is displayed. These sought-after culinary delights are among the first items that are sold. The hustle of activity at such a bazaar is reminiscent of the 'Martini-Markt' or the 'Christmas-Markts' that many recall from home.

Toward the end of the month the family festival of Thanksgiving, celebrated here in the United States, has become a new tradition for these transplanted Germans. Although it may recall memories of St. Martin celebrations, these Germans integrate their traditions by putting a turkey on the festive table at Thanksgiving and a beautiful stuffed goose at Christmas.

BETTELMANNPUDDING
(Begger's Pudding)

Kris Jeter

A recipe handwritten in German in my grandmother's 1912 cookbook.

1 soup bowl full of rye bread crumbs
1 cup (160 gr) currants   1 soup bowl full of sliced apples
  butter   sugar; cinnamon

Put a layer of breadcrumbs into a buttered pudding form; add a little butter and put apple slices on top. Add currants, sugar and cinnamon. Alternate these layers, ending with breadcrumbs and butter. Bake in a moderate (350°F) oven for one hour.

EIERSCHECK
(Egg Custard Cake)

Karoline Heusler

Prepare your favorite yeast dough recipe or try the one following used for this egg custard!

1 16 oz. container sour cream   ½ teaspoon vanilla extract
7 medium or 6 large eggs   ½ cup (1 stick) melted (but not warm)
⅓ cup (67 gr) sugar   butter

Mix thoroughly to a thick cream consistency. Pour this mixture over a thin layer of yeast dough (yeast dough should be prepared ahead). Bake in a 13x9½x2″ pan in preheated oven at 325° until the top has a golden color (30 - 45 minutes).

HEFETEIG
(Yeast Dough)

Karoline Heusler

5 cups (½ kg) flour   ¾ cup + 2 tablespoons (⅕ liter)
1 teaspoon salt   lukewarm milk
⅓ cup + 1 tablespoon (80 gr) sugar) 1-2 eggs
½ cup (100 gr) butter   2 cakes (about 25-30 gr) yeast
                                     rind of ½ lemon

Place flour into a slightly warmed bowl. Add sugar, salt, finely cut up butter, eggs, lemon rind and knead thoroughly. Add lukewarm milk as you knead. Let the dough rise, dust it with flour, cover it with a thin kitchen towel and set it in a warm draft free area (1 - 1½ hrs).

This dough can be used for a Napfkuchen, Bundt or yeast braid as well as for the foundation for Eierscheck - rolled out very thinly.

SCHOKOLADE BUISKUITROLLE   Elli Beck
(Chocolate Roll)

6 eggs (separated)	3 tablespoons cocoa
1 tablespoon flour	½ cup (100 gr) sugar
1 tablespoon cornstarch	¼ teaspoon baking powder

Beat egg yolks and sugar until creamy. Sift together flour, cornstarch, cocoa and baking powder and sift over cream mixture. Mix. Beat egg whites and then fold them under the cream mixture. Mix gently. On a cookie sheet with a one inch edge place wax paper over the entire sheet and grease the paper lightly. (I use oil; butter tends to burn.) Pour the mixture onto the sheet and spread out the dough. Bake at 350°F. for 20 - 25 minutes. After the cake has baked, take a moist kitchen linen towel and turn over cake onto the towel. Peel off the wax paper carefully and roll up cake with towel lengthwise and let it cool. In the meantime prepare one pint whipped cream with powdered sugar and vanilla. When cooled, unroll the chocolate roll and spread the whipped cream in between and roll up again (without towel!) Dust roll with powdered sugar and refrigerate until ready to serve.

Serves 12 - 14.

FRANZÖSISCHE WINDBEUTEL
MIT VANILLA SAUCE   Elli Beck
(Cream Puffs with Vanilla Sauce)

I have often served this to my family as a special dessert treat on cool days when I prepared vegetable soup as the main dish. They looked forward to this!

½ cup (118 ml) milk	dash salt
½ cup (118 ml) water	1 cup (115 gr) flour
1 stick (227 gr) butter	4 eggs

Heat milk and melt butter in it. Add all other ingredients and mix together with a wooden spoon. Let dough cool and then add 4 eggs, one at a time. Drop by teaspoonful into a pot with hot oil (or electric deep fryer) and fry a few seconds until golden brown. Remove, drain on a paper towel and dust with powdered sugar. Eat warm, plain or serve with a vanilla sauce.

SAUCE: Prepare vanilla pudding according to instructions on package. I usually double the amount of milk and prepare a thinner sauce. Spoon this over the cream puff.

REHRÜCKEN KUCHEN
Elisabeth Kottenhahn
(Saddle of Venison Cake)

The form of the cakepan gives this cake its name. It is baked in an elongated loafpan with a design in the bottom. When the almonds are stuck into the glaze, the cake looks like a saddle of venison, larded with strips of salt pork. This has become the favorite birthday cake of my husband, A. P. Kottenhahn.

10 tablespoons (150 gr) butter	2 teaspoons baking powder
⅞ cup (175 gr) sugar	½ cup (⅛ liter) milk
4 eggs	¾ cup (3.5 oz. or 100 gr) ground
4 oz. (100 gr) grated chocolate	hazelnuts
1¼ cups (150 gr) flour	chocolate glaze
1 package of chocolate pudding	slivered almonds

Cream butter, sugar and eggs. Add chocolate. Sift flour with baking powder; dissolve pudding in milk. Add flour and pudding alternately to batter. Mix well; add hazelnuts. (You may add 1 teaspoon Nescafe, ½ teaspoon cinnamon and a little nutmeg). Fill dough into greased 'Rehrücken-form' or bread loaf pan; bake at 350° for 50-55 minutes. Let sit for 10 minutes in pan. then turn out onto cooling rack and let cool. Cover with a chocolate glaze and stick slivered almonds into it.

HASELNUSSKUCHEN
Elisabeth Kottenhahn
(Hazelnut Cake)

Delicious for afternoon coffee hour for guests who appreciate something good!

9 oz. (250 gr) ground hazelnuts	2 cups (250 gr) powdered sugar
5 eggs, separated	rum

Cream egg yolks and sugar, add hazelnuts, a little rum and fold stiff egg whites into the batter. Bake slowly in moderate oven. (300°-325°) about 20 minutes. Dust with powdered sugar or glaze with chocolate glaze.

HASELNUSSTORTE
Elli Beck
(Hazelnut Torte)

My sister served this delicious torte to us on our recent trip to Germany. I brought the recipe back home and prepared it for the ladies in my local Kaffee Klatsch. It was a huge success!

1 stick (125 gr) butter
¾ cup (150 gr) sugar
1 teaspoon vanilla
2 eggs
4 oz. (125 gr) finely ground hazelnuts
1¾ cups (200 gr) flour

1 heaping teaspoon baking powder
½ cup (⅛ l) milk

Rum glaze:
½ cup (65 gr) powdered sugar
1 tablespoon rum (light or dark)

Cream butter, sugar, eggs and vanilla. Mix in hazelnuts. In a separate container mix together baking powder and flour and then add alternately with milk to the cream mixture. Grease a spring form and dust bottom and sides with bread crumbs. Pour torte dough into spring form and bake for 30-40 minutes at 350° F. When cake is baked turn it out immediately onto a serving plate and pour rum glaze over entire torte.
An alternate version: instead of rum glaze, prepare 2 cups of whipped cream. Cut torte in half and spread 1 cup cream between the two layers and spread 1 cup over the entire torte. Keep refrigerated until ready to serve!

BUTTER-ODER ZUCKERKUCHEN
(Butter or Sugar Cake)   Grete Braun

1½ cakes compressed yeast	Preheat oven on high for 5 min.
1 teaspoon sugar	
1 cup (237 ml) lukewarm milk	Topping:
4½ cups (500 gr) plain flour	½ cup (113 gr) butter
½ cup (100 gr) sugar	⅓ cup (70 gr) sugar
lemon rind grated from 1 lemon	½ cup (60 gr) almonds, chopped
1 pinch salt	cinnamon
¼ cup (60 gr) butter, melted	
2 eggs	Baking time 350° for 15 - 20 min.

Cream yeast with sugar and 5 tablespoons milk. Sieve ⅔ of the flour into a large mixing bowl, make a well in center and pour in yeast mixture. Cover with ¼ inch layer of flour, Distribute the sugar, lemon rind, melted butter, and eggs around the well. **Do not** allow to touch yeast. When flour covering yeast shows large cracks, stir all ingredients together, adding rest of milk. Beat the dough with a strong wooden spoon until bubbles appear. Knead in rest of flour, leave in warm place until doubled. Knead again, roll out on buttered baking sheet.
Topping: Cut butter evenly over dough (small pieces), mix sugar, cinnamon and nuts and sprinkle over cake - must rise again to double in size then bake - must bake to golden brown.
Other toppings can be used:
1. Sliced apple mixed with cinnamon, sugar, and rum.
2. Plums sliced, 3 eggs separated, 4 tablespoons sugar, 3 tablespoons sour cream. Beat egg yolks and sugar until frothy, add sour cream and stiffly beaten egg whites and pour over sliced plums.

GEWÜRZKUCHEN
(Spicecake)

Elisabeth Kottenhahn

from grandmother Marx

½ cup (125 gr) butter	1 teaspoon ground cloves
1½ cups (300 gr) sugar	1 teaspoon ground cinnamon
2-4 eggs, separated	1 teaspoon vanilla
2½ cups (350 gr) flour	1 teaspoon ground nutmeg
3½ teaspoons baking powder	1 cup (¼ liter) milk
6 tablespoons (60 gr) cocoa	

Cream butter, add sugar and egg yolks. Mix well., Sift flour with spices and cocoa and add to batter, alternating with milk. Fold in stiffly beaten egg whites. Fill batter in greased loaf pan and bake at 350°F for about an hour. Serve with 'lots of whipped cream'!

SCHLESISCHER STREUSELKUCHEN
(Silesian Crumb Cake)

Elli Beck

	Filling:
4 cups (454 gr) flour	12 oz. (336 gr) cottage cheese
1 stick (227 gr) butter	1 egg
1 cup milk	3 tablespoons sugar
1 egg	vanilla
5 tablespoons sugar	
¼ cup water	
1 package dry yeast	
1 lemon rind	

Put flour into large bowl. Sprinkle yeast into another container with luke-warm water and let sit for 15 minutes until it bubbles. In another pot heat milk, butter, sugar, salt until lukewarm and pour over flour. Add yeast mixture, lemon rind and egg to flour. Mix dough and then let rise in a warm place to double in bulk. Roll out onto a cookie sheet and bring dough up on edge of sheet. Mix cottage cheese filling ingredients together and spread over yeast dough. Add the following crumb recipe:

1 cup (227 gr) sweet butter	½ teaspoon cinnamon
1 cup (200 gr) sugar	3½ cups (400 gr) flour
1 teaspoon vanilla	

Mix crumb ingredients together in a bowl by hand until they form a pea-size crumb-like consistency. Sprinkle over the cottage cheese filling and let rise for 30 minutes. Bake at 350° F. for 25 minutes until a golden yellow. This cake also freezes well and can be baked ahead for company. It tastes as fresh as ever!

STREUSELKUCHEN
(Crumb Cake)

Anna Herold

This is an easy cake to bake and is one that I often made for Sunday. If company didn't stop by, the cake didn't last too long anyway with four boys in the house. It's still a favorite today with relatives and grandchildren.

2½ cups (290 gr) flour
2 teaspoons baking powder
  pinch of salt
¼ lb. (113 gr) butter
¼ lb. (113 gr) oleo
1 cup (200 gr) sugar

3 eggs
1 teaspoon vanilla
½ teaspoon lemon extract or grated rind
  of 1 lemon
3 tablespoons milk

Mix together butter, oleo and sugar until creamy. Add eggs one at a time and beat thoroughly. Add vanilla and lemon. Mix together flour, baking powder and salt and then add gradually to butter mixture. Add milk and beat thoroughly. Spread on a cookie sheet (11½ in. x 17½ in. pan with an edge all around). Spread crumbs on top of cake and bake 25-30 minutes at 350°.

Crumbs:
¼ lb. (113 gr) butter
½ cup (100 gr) sugar
1 cup (115 gr) flour

Mix ingredients together by hand in a bowl until they form a lumpy or crumbly consistency. Add more flour if mixture appears too moist. Spread over cake and bake.

KAFFEEKUCHEN
(Coffee Cake)

Emilie Toman

This is a fast and easy recipe.

½ cup (113 gr) butter
1 cup (200 gr) sugar
2 eggs
3 cups (345 gr) flour

rind of 1 lemon
3 teaspoons baking powder
1 cup (237 ml) milk

Cream butter, add sugar, eggs and lemon rind. Add flour and baking powder alternately with milk. Mix well until creamy. Spread on baking sheet (with rim), sprinkle crumb mixture evenly on top of cake. Bake at 350° for 30 - 40 minutes.

Crumbs:
1 tablespoon flour
½ cup (100 gr) sugar

2 tablespoons butter
  cinnamon

Cream butter and sugar together, add flour and cinnamon and work into a crumbly consistency. Spread on top of cake.

KAFFEEKUCHEN

Fannie Kummer

(German Coffee Cake)

This was taken from an old cookbook belonging to my grandmother. It was handwritten and is quite old; one she enjoyed baking when she was first married around 1893.　　　　　　　　　　Alma M. DeMott

Dissolve two cakes of yeast in ½ pint (1 cup or 237 ml) of lukewarm milk and when thoroughly dissolved, add ½ pint of lukewarm water. Take about 1¾ lbs. (7 cups or 800 gr) sifted flour and with it and liquid containing dissolved yeast make a sponge. Set sponge to rise in moderately warm draught free area and cover with a cloth. The sponge will be ready in about 1½ to 2 hours according to temperature of room. Just before sponge is ready, rub together 3 ounces (6 tablespoons or 90 gr) of butter and 3 ounces (½ cup or 100 gr) of sugar and beat same until quite light. Add to beaten butter and sugar two eggs beaten well and ½ teaspoon of salt and mix all together. Add this mixture to sponge to make a soft dough, so soft that it can be lifted with a spoon and dropped into baking pans. Grease pans or mold (a Bundt or baking ring mold type) thoroughly and half fill with dough. Set in a warm place free from draughts to rise; when pans are ¾ filled, bake in a moderately hot oven. A few raisins may be added if desired.

This recipe will make three medium sized cakes.

KAFFEEKUCHEN

Grace Strohmann

(Brown Sugar Coffee Cake)

Mother made this for Sunday breakfast before we went to church. It makes up very easily and is a family recipe handed down from my grandmother, Fannie Kummer.　　　　　　　　　　Alma M. DeMott

2 cups (400 gr) brown sugar	2 eggs
2 tablespoons butter	2 cups (474 ml) milk
4 cups (460 gr) flour	½ teaspoon salt
4 teaspoons baking powder	

Topping:

4 tablespoons butter	8 tablespoons flour
4 tablespoons granulated sugar	2 teaspoons cinnamon

Mix together all ingredients; brush top of cake with milk or melted butter before putting on the crumbs. Bake in a long shallow baking pan in a moderate oven (350°F) about 30 minutes.

This makes 2 cakes.

GESUNDHEITSKUCHEN
Trudy Van Oot
(Health Cake)

1¼ cups (2½ sticks or 285 gr) butter or margarine
2¼ cups (250 gr) sugar   2½ teaspoons vanilla or lemon extract
  7 eggs   2 tablespoons lemon or orange bits (optional)
2½ cups (290 gr) flour

Preheat oven to 325°. Grease and flour dust a Bundt cake pan. With electric mixer cream sugar and butter till foamy and smooth. Add eggs, one at a time, beating after each one. Add flour all at once, then flavoring. Beat till batter is smooth and almost foamy. Pour into pan and bake (middle rack) for 50 - 60 minutes or until done. Cool 10 minutes on rack. Dust with powdered sugar or dribble icing. (to your liking) over it.

KÖNIGSKUCHEN
Anna Herold
(Royal Cake)

1 cup (227 gr) butter   4 cups (460 gr) sifted flour
1 cup (200 gr) sugar   4 teaspoons baking powder, pinch of salt
4-5 eggs   ½ cup (118 ml) milk or little more
2 tablespoons rum   1½ cups (250 gr or 350 ml) raisins
  juice and grated rind of ½ lemon   both white and dark
1 teaspoon almond extract   ½ cup (100 gr) candied red cherries as
                                                            desirable

Preheat oven to 350°. Cream butter and sugar until light and fluffy. Beat in eggs one at a time with mixer until well blended. Mix in rum, lemon juice and rind and almond extract. Sift flour with baking powder and salt. Add flour and milk alternately and gradually to butter and eggs mixing well. Do not add too much milk. The batter should be firm and heavy. Fold in raisins and cherries. Butter a large loaf pan or large round angel food pan and sprinkle with flour or bread crumbs on sides and bottom. Turn batter into pan and bake about 1¼ to 1½ hours. Cake may be cooled in pan.

MARMORGUGELHUPF
(Marble Bundt Cake)

Gardy Epp

2 sticks + 2 tablespoons (252 gr) butter or margarine
1 cup (200 gr) sugar
4 eggs
  dash of salt
1 teaspoon vanilla
2 tablespoons rum
3 cups (345 gr) flour

4 teaspoons baking powder
⅔ cup (160 ml) milk
3 tablespoons cocoa
1 tablespoon sugar
2-3 tablespoons milk

Cream the butter and gradually add the sugar, eggs and flavorings. Mix and sieve the flour and baking powder. Then stir flour and milk alternately into the creamed mixture until a firm consistency is obtained. Grease and dust a special gugelhupf pan (available in gourmet cookware stores) with bread crumbs or use a 12-cup Bundt pan. Fill ⅔ of the mixture into the prepared pan. Stir the cocoa, sugar and milk into the remaining mixture. Place the chocolate mixture on top of the light mixture already in the pan and swirl together with a fork. Bake at 350° for 50 to 60 minutes. When the cake is cooled, dribble a chocolate glaze over the cake or dust with powdered sugar.

KUGELHUPF
(Bundt Cake)

Leni Holzhauser

2 tablespoons sugar
1 envelope yeast
¼ cup (59 ml) warm milk
1½ sticks + 1 tablespoon (185 gr) butter
½ cup (65 gr) confectioner's sugar
3 egg yolks

2 ⅔ cups (300 gr) flour
¼ teaspoon salt
¾ cup (178 ml) milk
¾ cup (185 gr) raisins
  grated rind of ½ lemon
½ cup (60 gr) slivered almonds

In a small bowl combine 2 tablespoons sugar, 1 envelope active yeast, and ¼ cup warm milk and let the mixture stand for 10 minutes. In a bowl beat 1½ sticks (¾ cup) plus 1 tablespoon butter with ½ cup confectioner's sugar until the mixture is fluffy. Beat in 3 egg yolks and the yeast mixture. Sift 2⅔ cups flour with ¼ teaspoon salt and add it alternately with ¾ cup milk. Beat the dough for 10 minutes or until it is smooth and elastic. Stir in ¾ cup raisins and the grated rind of ½ lemon. Brush well a 6-cup tube pan or Kugelhupf mold with melted butter and dust it lightly with flour. Distribute ½ cup slivered blanched almonds around the bottom of the mold. Pour the dough into the mold, cover it and let it rise in a warm place for 1 to 1½ hours. Bake the Kugelhupf in a hot oven (400°) for 10 minutes and reduce the heat to moderate (350°) and bake it for 30 to 35 minutes or until it is golden. Let the Kugelhupf cool in the mold for 10 minutes and unmold it on a cake rack. Sprinkle with sifted confectioner's sugar and let it cool completely. Sprinkle the Kugelhupf again before serving.

BIENENSTICH
(Honey Bee Cake)

Erika Schirm

Rich Yeast Dough:

3½ cups (400 gr) flour
1 package dry yeast
1 cup (237 ml) milk
½ cup (113 gr) butter or margarine

¼ cup (50 gr) sugar
1 teaspoon salt
1 egg

In a large bowl combine 2 cups flour and yeast. Heat milk, butter, salt, sugar till warm, stirring to melt butter. Add to dry mixture, add egg. Beat at low speed ½ min. Beat 3 minutes at high speed. By hand stir in enough of remaining flour to make a stiff dough. Turn into greased bowl, cover and let rise till double (1½ hrs.). Turn on floured surface. Divide in half.

Makes two Zimt-Nusskuchen or one 2-layered Bienenstich.

Almond Syrup:

½ cup (113 gr) butter or margarine
1 cup (200 gr) sugar
1 tablespoon milk
1 teaspoon lemon juice

¾ cup (90 gr) sliced
  blanched almonds
½ teaspoon vanilla

In a saucepan, melt the ¼ cup butter. Add sugar, 1 tablespoon milk and lemon juice. Bring to boil, stirring constantly. Remove from heat; stir in almonds and ½ teaspoon vanilla. Set aside to cool.

On lightly floured surface, roll out the ½ dough to 13" x 9" rectangles. Carefully fit dough into a well-greased 13" x 9" x 2" baking pan. Spread cool almond syrup over dough. Cover, let rise in warm place till double (1 hour). Bake at 375° for 15-20 minutes. Cool 10 minutes, remove from pan, cool on rack.

Vanilla Creme Filling:

¼ cup (50 gr) sugar
2 tablespoons cornstarch
  dash of salt
¾ cup (178 ml) milk

1 beaten egg
½ teaspoon vanilla
¾ cup (170 gr) butter
  or margarine

In saucepan combine ¼ cup sugar, cornstarch and salt. Gradually add the ¾ cup milk. Cook over medium heat till mixture thickens and bubbles. Cook 2 or 3 minutes. Stir some of mixture into beaten egg; return to mixture. Cook. Cool. Add vanilla. Cover with waxed paper. Cream remaining butter. Beat cooled pudding into butter. Chill at least 30 minutes. Cut baked cake dough into 3 inch squares. Split each piece horizontally and fill with creme filling.

Makes 12 servings.

BIENENSTICH
(Bee Sting or Honey Bee Cake)

Johanna Rosselli

Yeast Dough:

3 packages dry yeast
1 cup (¼ liter) milk
6½ cups (750 gr) flour
¾ cup (175 gr) butter
⅔ cup (125 gr) sugar

1 package vanillin sugar (available in gourmet shops) or 1 teaspoon vanilla
2 eggs
salt

Filling:

14 oz. (400 gr) chopped almonds
1 lb. (500 gr) butter
2 cups (400 gr) sugar

Dissolve yeast in 3 tablespoons warm milk. Set aside. Mix flour, ½ cup (125 gr) melted butter, sugar, vanillin sugar, eggs and salt. Add yeast mixture. Mix well. Cover bowl with a moist towel and let dough rise in a warm place. Roll out dough onto a greased cookie sheet, let rise again. Melt the rest of the butter and brush the dough with it. Prick the dough with a fork. For the filling melt the butter, add sugar and boil shortly. Stir in almonds, remove from flame. Let cool. Spread over dough and bake in moderate oven (350°F) until brown.

ROTWEINKUCHEN
(Red Wine Cake)

Irmgard Stiffel

1 cup + 2 tablespoons (250 gr) butter or margarine
1¼ cups (250 gr) sugar
4 eggs
2 cups (250 gr) flour
2½ teaspoons (1 package) baking powder
1 package vanillin sugar (available in gourmet shops) or 1 teaspoon vanilla

1 teaspoon cinnamon
1 teaspoon cocoa
3½ oz. (100 gr) chocolate 'streusel' - (jimmies)
½ cup (⅛ liter) red wine

Mix butter, sugar and vanillin sugar to a creamy consistency; gradually add eggs separately. Sift flour and baking powder together and add gradually to butter mixture. Add red wine slowly and mix well; then add cinnamon, cocoa and lastly the chocolate jimmies. Pour into a greased springform and bake 45-60 minutes at 350-375°F. Dribble a lemon glaze icing over the cooled cake.

MOHNKUCHEN
(Poppy Seed Cake)

Beatrix Tannian

Poppy Seed Cake is a favorite cake among friends and is an easy cake to bake and take along. I use the prepared filling as a short-cut and I find it very delicious!

Prepare dough by the kneading method or if preferable, use a yeast dough. If you do not have a favorite or special dough, the following is suggested:

1½ cups (170 gr) flour
⅓ cup (70 gr) sugar
½ cup (100 gr) butter or margarine
pinch of baking powder
1 package Oetker vanillin sugar (available in gourmet shops) or 1 teaspoon vanilla

Filling:
1 jar Baker's Poppy Seed Filling

Sift together flour and baking powder in a bowl. Make a well in the center, add sugar and vanillin sugar. Add cold butter, cut into small pieces. Cover with flour and starting from the center, knead all ingredients quickly with the hands into a smooth ball. Roll out into a rectangular shape about ⅜'' thick. Spread Baker's Poppy Seed Filling over the surface of the dough. Roll up dough into a long roll and shape it to form a circle (don't join two ends). Place on cookie sheet, baste entire cake with a beaten egg yolk. Bake at 350° for 30 minutes until it has a golden color and a toothpick comes out clean.

For variety, a nut filling is suggested. Mix together 1½ cups (200 gr) ground walnuts, ½ cup (100 gr) sugar, 1 teaspoon cinnamon, few drops almond extract and 1 egg white beaten. Spread this over the dough and follow above directions.

ZITRONEN TEE BROT
(Lemon Tea Bread)

Alma M. DeMott

This is a good dessert bread which keeps well and can be frozen.

1 egg
1½ cups (300 gr) sugar
juice of ½ lemon
3 cups (350 gr) flour
1 cup (237 ml) milk
3 teaspoons baking powder
¼ teaspoon nutmeg
chopped rind of 2 large lemons

Put together in order given, beating well after each addition. The simplest way to prepare the lemon is to shave off only the yellow part of the rind before the juice has been squeezed out; the inner thick white skin gives a bitter taste. Put the yellow rind through the food chopper twice and fold in last of all. When mixed the dough should be a trifle heavier than for cakes, as it gives a finer texture. Bake in a well-greased loaf pan in a slow oven for one hour.

This is easily put together as there is no shortening to bother with and it is inexpensive. Nuts may be used as a variation, with or without the lemon; orange peel is not as successful. If by any chance there is any left over, try it toasted.

MOHNSTRIETZEL
(Poppyseed Cake)

Johanna Rosselli

Yeast Dough:

2 packages yeast, dissolved in
1 cup (¼ liter) warm milk
4¼ cups (500 gr) flour
⅓ cup (60 gr) sugar

¼ cup (60 gr) butter
grated lemon rind
1 egg
salt

Dissolve yeast in milk; set aside. Mix flour, melted butter, sugar, lemon rind, egg and salt. Add yeast mixture and mix well. Cover bowl with a moist towel and let dough rise in a warm place.

Filling:

½ lb. (250 gr) ground poppyseeds
1 cup (¼ liter) milk
3 tablespoons (40 gr) butter
¼ cup (25 gr) almonds
1 cup (200 gr) sugar
Glaze:
3 tablespoons butter
powdered sugar

¼ cup (60 gr) white raisins
1 egg
cinnamon
breadcrumbs

Bring the milk to boiling point, pour over the ground poppyseeds. Add melted butter, sugar, almonds, raisins, egg and cinnamon. If too soft, add some breadcrumbs. Roll the yeast dough into a 1 cm. thick rectangle. Spread filling over it close to the edges. Roll into long roll. Put with seam facing down onto greased cookie sheet, let rise again (covered with towel) brush with melted butter and bake in 350°F. oven for about one hour.

NUSSBROT
(Nut Bread)

Alma M. DeMott

Mother taught us girls how to bake starting with this recipe. It's an old family recipe.

1 egg
¾ cup (150 gr) sugar
1 teaspoon (scant) salt
1 cup (237 ml) sweet milk

2 teaspoons baking powder
3½ cups (400 gr) flour-sifted twice
1 cup (120 gr) chopped walnuts

Mix egg, sugar and milk. Add flour, salt, baking powder and nuts to first mixture. Mix well and bake at least one hour at 350°F.

SCHWARZWÄLDERKIRSCHTORTE
(Black Forest Cherry Cake)   Trudy Gilgenast

A very special cake and a favorite of my family and friends is the Black Forest Cherry Cake. I prepare it a day ahead and allow it 'to set' in the refrigerator overnight. It tastes better, too, and this permits the kirsch in the cake and whipped cream to permeate and make the dessert especially delicious. I have served it for afternoon coffee although it has also become a birthday cake as well as a dessert for special occasions.

Cake

Use a favorite chocolate sponge cake recipe and bake two 9 inch layers. (I use Duncan Hines Devil's Food Cake.) Sprinkle each layer with 1 tablespoon Kirschwasser. Cut each layer in half horizontally. Spread chocolate butter cream filling between the layers. Over the filling of the second layer arrange 1½ cups drained and halved dark, sweet, pitted cherries (1 lb. 5 oz. can). Reserve about 10-12 whole cherries for decoration on top. Place the third and fourth layers on top. (I find that I have to hold these layers together with toothpicks and set the cake into the refrigerator for ½ hr. to allow it to set before I can complete the sides).

Spread top and sides with a Kirschwasser flavored whipped cream. Top with chocolate curls (also around sides) and garnish top with the reserved cherries. The curls can be made from 1 oz. semi-sweet baking chocolate. Use a vegetable peeler to shave the chocolate curls.

Chocolate Butter Cream Filling

5 egg yolks	1 cup (227 gr) sweet butter
⅔ cup (130 gr) sugar	3 oz. (85 gr) melted semi-sweet
⅓ cup (80 ml) water	chocolate
	3 tablespoons Kirschwasser

Beat egg yolks lightly. Set aside. Bring to boil sugar and water. Stir only until sugar dissolves. Cook until a little dropped in cold water forms a soft ball (238°F). Pour the boiling hot syrup very slowly, in a thin stream, over the beaten yolks, beating vigorously until thick. Beat in, a little at a time, the sweet butter, softened. Add the melted semi-sweet chocolate and Kirschwasser. Chill until thick enough to spread. (I usually make this ahead and let it set overnight in the refrigerator — before putting the cake together.) Makes about 2 cups.

Whipped Cream:

1½ cups (355 ml) heavy cream
⅓ cup (45 gr) confectioners sugar
2-3 tablespoons Kirschwasser

Beat cream adding confectioners sugar gradually and then the Kirschwasser. (If you add 1 teaspoon gelatin moistened with 1 tablespoon Kirschwasser which is placed over hot water to dissolve, to the whipped cream, it will help to keep it firm.)

SCHWARZWÄLDERKIRSCHTORTE
(Black Forest Cherry Cake) Gudrun McGee

Dough:
½ cup (100 gr) butter or margarine
½ cup (100 gr) sugar
1 package vanillin sugar (available in gourmet shops) or 1 teaspoon vanilla
4 eggs
⅔ cup (75 gr) almonds (ground)
3½ oz. (100 gr) chocolate (ground)
⅓ cup (50 gr) cornstarch
⅓ cup (50 gr) flour
2 teaspoons baking powder

Filling:
6-7 tablespoons Kirschwasser (cherry Schnaps)
1 cup (200 gr) marmalade preserves
or
1¼ cups (500 gr) sour cherries (light red cherries) pitted
2 cups (½ liter) whipped cream

Garnish:
chocolate shavings and cherries

Beat butter or margarine until foamy and slowly add sugar and vanillin sugar. Slowly add eggs and beat until substance is smooth. Then add the ground almonds and chocolate and finally the cornstarch mixed with the flour and baking powder. Put dough into a well-greased baking form (round, 24 cm. diameter and 5 cm. high) and bake at 350° for 40-50 minutes. When cake has cooled after baking, cut it into 3 layers. Sprinkle the bottom layer with cherry schnaps and then cover it with preserves or pitted cherries and top the cherries with some whipped cream. Place the middle layer on top, again sprinkle it with cherry schnaps and cover it with whipped cream. Put the top layer on, again sprinkle with cherry schnaps, cover with whipped cream and top with cherries and chocolate shavings (also cover sides of cake with whipped cream and chocolate shavings.)

SCHWARZWÄLDERKIRSCHTORTE
(Black Forest Cherry Cake) Gardy Epp

7 tablespoons (100 gr) butter or margarine
½ cup (100 gr) sugar
1 teaspoon vanilla
4 medium eggs
¾ cup (90 gr) ground almonds
¼ cup (60 ml or 30 gr) cocoa
or shredded chocolate
⅓ cup (50 gr) cornstarch
⅓ cup (50 gr) flour
2 teaspoons baking powder

Filling:

6 tablespoons Kirschwasser	1 package Whip It
1 lb. (454 gr) canned pitted cherries	(available in German specialty stores)
1 tablespoon cornstarch	1 teaspoon vanilla
2 cups (474 ml) whipping cream	sugar to taste
	shredded chocolate

Beat the butter until creamy and slowly add the sugar and vanilla. Then stir in the eggs, one at a time. Next mix in the almonds and cocoa or shredded chocolate. Sift together the flour, cornstarch and baking powder. Sift this mixture over the butter mixture and stir together. Turn the batter into a greased 8-inch springform and bake at 350° about 45 minutes. When done, allow to cool and cut into two layers. In the meantime, reserve 3 tablespoons of the cherry juice in a glass, pour the remaining cherries and juice (except for a few cherries reserved for decoration) into a saucepan and heat. Mix the cornstarch with the reserved cherry juice and pour into the saucepan with cherries. Bring to a boil while stirring. Then allow to cool.

To assemble the cake, sprinkle the bottom layer with 3 tablespoons of Kirschwasser. Spread the cooled cherries over the cake. Whip the cream in a large mixing bowl and add the Whip-It according to package directions. When the cream is almost stiff, add the vanilla and sugar to taste. Spread part of the whipped cream over the cherries. Place the other layer on top and sprinkle with the remaining Kirschwasser. Spread the top and sides with the remaining whipped cream. Sprinkle some shredded chocolate over the whipped cream and decorate with a few reserved cherries.

Serves 12.

LIEGNITZER BOMBE
(Liegnitz Bombe)

Eugenia Slavov

1¼ cups (500 gr) honey	5 oz. (150 gr) coarsely chopped almonds
1¼ cups (250 gr) sugar	6 bitter almonds
1 cup + 2 tablespoons (250 gr) butter	9 oz. (250 gr) grated chocolate
grated rind of 1 lemon	5 oz. (150 gr) finely chopped citrus
1 teaspoon cinnamon	1½ cups (9 oz. or 250 gr) currants
1 teaspoon finely ground cloves	2 tablespoons rum
6½ cups (750 gr) flour	1 teaspoon baking soda
2 eggs	

Heat together honey, sugar and butter to boiling point, mix thoroughly. Add lemon rind, cinnamon and cloves. Allow mixture to cool. To this mixture add flour, eggs, coarsely chopped almonds, bitter almonds, grated chocolate, citrus, currants and rum. Add 1 teaspoon of baking soda mixed with 1 cup lukewarm water. Place in a greased, floured, deep cake pan (or spring form) and bake at 350° for 45 minutes. After cake has cooled cover with a chocolate icing.

LINZER TORTE
(Linzer Torte)

Magda Ruoff

2 cups (227 gr) flour
1 cup (227 gr) sugar
8 oz. (227 gr) ground almonds
  or hazelnuts
1 cup (227 gr) butter

1 egg
½ teaspoon cinnamon
  pinch of powdered cloves
¾-1 cup (8 oz. or 227 gr) rasperry jam

Put flour onto a table (or onto a board or into a wide bowl), cut in butter and add sugar and egg. Use two knives, a pastry blender or your fingers and work into a nice dough. Refrigerate ½ hour. Then roll out ⅔ of dough and put into a springform. Press in a high edge and fill in jam. Then form small roll, strips of remainder of dough and create a lattice of 1 inch squares on top. Bake at 375° for approx. 45 minutes.

LINZER TORTE
(Linzer Torte)

Anke Becker

10 tablespoons (150 gr) butter
1¼ cups (250 gr) sugar
1 egg
1 tablespoon cinnamon, ground
½ teaspoon cloves, ground
  rind of ½ lemon, grated

1 tablespoon Schnaps (cherry - Kirsch)
1 cup (125 gr) almonds
1 cup + 1 tablespoon (125 gr) flour
3 teaspoons baking powder
¼ cup (1/16 liter) milk

Filling:
Marmalade (about 1 cup raspberry jam)

Mix all ingredients thoroughly. Spread ⅔ of the dough in buttered round pan. Put marmalade on top. Arrange rest of dough on top in rows in a lattice fashion and put some egg yolk mixed with milk on top. Bake at 400° F. for 45 minutes.

MALAKOWTORTE
(Malakow Torte)

Elli Beck

2¼ cups (½ l) milk
1 package (cooked) vanilla pudding
5 tablespoons sugar
½ lb. (227 gr) sweet butter
3 tablespoons powdered sugar

250 gr lady fingers
  (approximately 2 packages or 24)
6 tablespoons rum
½ cup (50 gr) currant jelly
  (approximately ½ of small jar)
3½ oz (100 gr) sliced almonds

Prepare pudding according to package directions and let cool. Whip butter with powdered sugar and add to cooled pudding mixture. Place ring of a spring form on a cake plate (serving plate) and line bottom with lady fingers. Put ½ of rum on the lady fingers; heat jam to a liquid and dab onto each lady finger. Then spread ½ of butter cream mixture over that. Repeat the rum, jam, butter cream layers. Save some of butter cream. Decorate with almonds and set in refrigerator to cool and set. After 1 hour remove spring form ring and spread butter cream around edge of cake and decorate with almonds. Tastes best when made the day before you serve it; keep in refrigerator. (I also roast the almonds in 1 tablespoon butter before sprinkling over cake; it gives an added flavor!)

ADVENT, SANKT NIKOLAUS, WEIHNACHTEN
(Advent, Saint Nicholas, Christmas)

An electricity fills the air toward the end of the calendar year and the beginning of the church year. With the season of Advent, four Sundays prior to Christmas, and the approach of the holiday season there is an atmosphere of anticipation and a hustle and bustle as preparations begin for the numerous festive occasions at this time of the year.

Of all the German holidays Christmas is the most cherished and remembered. Special family customs and traditions are still maintained by local Germans, for this is truly the most beautiful season of all. Within the intimate circle of family and close friends there is an atmosphere of serenity and a bond of love; for the German, Christmas is primarily a family affair; he doesn't celebrate with the usual open house and large party activities of the American. To many this was the greatest 'cultural shock' in adjusting to the new home.

The season begins with Advent, those four weeks which herald the birth of Christ, and the preparation of the wreath. Many families still prefer to make their own, some use ready-made wreaths, others use the wooden base and attach green branches. The wreath is made of fir branches and is interlaced with red ribbons. It holds four candles and is usually placed on a coffee table in the living room. Then, on the first Sunday of Advent the first candle is lit with family members and occasional invited friends participating. The afternoon coffee table is set in a more festive manner for this special celebration. A brief lighting ceremony takes place first, so that coffee, tea and baked goods can be enjoyed in the glow of this first candle. Selections from the Bible are read and verses or poems are spoken or read. Singing and music are important elements in celebrating all aspects of the German Christmas. In most households family members perform on piano, violin, horn, accordian or guitar. Similar ceremonies follow during the next weeks until all four candles are lit. The big moment is approaching quickly, anticipation mounts and points the way to the many lights of the Christmas tree which are to appear in a few more days.

This season is an especially festive one for children who are excited about the preparations and surprises. The Advent calendar, depicting a myriad of religious and secular pictures, brings shrieks of joy each day when a new window is opened. There are 24 windows in all leading to Christmas Eve. There are also more elaborate calendars today which offer a piece of chocolate candy behind each opening. Such enticement makes it doubly difficult to avoid peeking and opening future windows too soon!

Another special day for children early in the Advent season is Saint Nicholas Day on December 6. This day commemorates Bishop Nicholas of Myra in Asia Minor, about whom many miracles are reported. He is known as the patron saint of mariners and of students. In modern practice the Nicholas visit is the real beginning of the Christmas celebration. Children put their shoes at the end of the bed, on a bench or outside the bedroom door or hang a long stocking in anticipation of lots of goodies. In a local kindergarten class the children also put out a shoe in hopes that Nicholas will find their room. The good children receive nuts, candy and fruit; the naughty receive a stick or switch. This custom parallels our hanging a stocking on Christmas Eve so that Santa Claus will fill it with special goodies. In some regions of Germany St. Nicholas is accompanied by 'Knecht Ruprecht' (servant Ruprecht) who admonishes the children who have not behaved. Since it is St. Nicholas who brings small gifts for children early in the season, many Germans refer to the bearer of gifts on Christmas Eve as the Christ Child, others refer to the 'Weihnachtsmann' (Christmas Man) or Santa Claus.

Another event of excitement and pleasure for grownups and children alike is the Christmas fair. Everyone is mobilized for a family visit to the fair where bright and shining rows of stalls and booths are set against the picturesque market or cathedral square. The most famous of these fairs is the Christkindlesmarkt in Nuremberg. Here are found stalls with a thousand and one glittering ornaments for the tree; other stalls offer finely-carved creche figures and the beautiful Nuremberg angel used to adorn the crown of the tree. Most fascinating are the toy stalls which display music boxes, 'Räuchermännchen' (smoking men), nutcrackers, beautiful pyramids and doll houses. Such an outing truly affords fun and exitement for the entire family and inspires the making of natural decorations for the house and the tree. In later years it brings back memories of that special event on a cold, snowy December day.

Finally the long awaited day arrives — Christmas Eve. Shops and offices close at noon in Germany and everyone completes preparations for the family celebration and the official two day holiday on December 25 and 26. The Germans whose roots have been transplanted also continue their customs on the holiest of eves.

Depending on the time of church services families attend together at 6:00 p.m. or later at candlelight services or midnight mass to express their joy at this season and to hear again the familiar Christmas message.

A light supper is usually eaten before or after the tree trimming and gift exchange activities are begun. A variety of Wursts (sausages) are popular at this time and are served occasionally with mashed potatoes but more frequently with potato salad. Herring salad recipes vary; however, this dish is a must on Christmas Eve. Some salads are prepared with sour cream, others contain beets or pickles. 'Karpfen in Blau' (carp in blue) is another delicacy served in some homes, scallops or cheese fondue in others. 'Glühwein' (spiced wine) or wine are popular beverages with a festive flavor. Finally the numerous cookies that have been baked for weeks and stored for this special holiday are brought out and served. Everyone has his favorite kind from the assortment which include: Springerle, Lebkuchen, Spritz, Zimtsterne, and many others. Every housewife has her favorite cookie recipes and some also have a special recipe for the Christmas bread or 'Weihnachtsstollen'. These recipes vary as to region as well as to family secrets.

The 'Bunter Teller', (plate of colorful mixed goodies), is another custom still practiced in some families. Each family member receives a plate filled with colorful cookies, nuts, candies, fruits and other special delights.

Finally, and in many homes not until this evening is the live tree brought into the house. Some decorate together as a family, others permit the children to see the tree only after the ringing of a bell is heard announcing the departure of the 'Christkind' who has delivered the gifts. Until that time preparations are done in secret and the anticipation of surprise and joy continues to mount. For young and old alike there is a moment of surprise when the lights are all turned off and the doors are thrown open to reveal the beautifully decorated tree in all its lighted splendor! It is then that the intimate family unit enjoys the wondrous magic of Christmas with the fragrance of a pine or fir tree wafting through the room and the dancing shadows of real wax candles casting a warm glow across radiant faces. The love and togetherness of this evening is truly a magical and unforgettable experience. Before the gifts are exchanged and opened, the group joins in the singing of carols and many accompany the singing on various musical insruments. There is the reading of the Christmas story from the Bible and children have to present a poem which they have been memorizing for weeks. The gifts are then distributed and the final moment of anticipation and surprise has arrived. Amid shouts of laughter, the rustle of wrapping paper, cracking of nuts, the ringing of the church bells and the singing of 'Stille Nacht, Heilige Nacht' this sacred evening slips away to memories.

Christmas day is also a festive but more quiet one and is spent visiting or entertaining relatives and friends. Some families, however, do leave the gift exchange until the morning and celebrate with a special breakfast afterwards. In this way they solve the dilemma of 'Christkind' versus Santa Claus. The 'Christkind' brings the tree and the story is read in its honor. The primarily homemade gifts are laid under the tree to be opened the next morning along with the stockings which Santa Claus filled that night. Thus both the German and the American customs are interwoven and enjoyed.

In most homes the dinner consists of goose or turkey with other favorite dishes to complement the meat. It is the one time of the year when eating and drinking seem to continue forever, for there are a wealth and abundance of culinary delights.

Christmas is a celebration for everyone and brings the message of 'Peace on Earth, Good Will Toward Men'. It is a special season of reaching out to one another, for its traditions and customs literally bring families and friends together from all over the world. Whenever and wherever possible relatives and loved ones will travel great distances to spend 'Heilig Abend' (Holy Eve) together once again.

GEBRATENE GANS
Ingeborg Keith
(Roast Goose with Meat Stuffing)

This is the recipe which has become our traditional Christmas dinner.

Preheat oven to 325°. Prick skin of goose all over with a fork. Put goose into oven for approx. 45 minutes, which allows some of the grease to cook out. Let goose cool off before filling with stuffing. Roast goose (8 - 10 lbs.) uncovered for approx. 3 hours. Skim off grease from time to time and baste goose occasionally with drippings. Make gravy from drippings. Serve with applesauce and mashed potatoes.

Stuffing:

1 lb (454 gr) ground beef	1 egg
10-12 slices of white bread	salt and pepper to taste
1 chopped onion	chopped giblets (uncooked)

Remove crust from bread and cut slices into small pieces. Moisten bread with water, squeeze out excess water. Mix all ingredients and stuff cavity of goose loosely.

GEBRATENE GANS UND ENTE
(Roast Goose and Duck)

Sophia Kopec

Preheat oven for 15 minutes at 450°F. Prepare fowl for roasting. Smear with garlic, paprika, salt with hands all over the outside. Stuff inside with fresh diced apple, prunes, apricots or dried fruit. Prick bird with toothpick or fork and put into oven. Put bird in oven for 30 minutes at 450° uncovered and without water. Turn to 350° and roast for 30 minutes, then cover and bake for one hour. Uncover, pour off liquid and roast 15 minutes on each side at 450°. Prick skin and baste while roasting.

APFEL IM SCHLAFROCK
(Apple in a Blanket)

Elisabeth Kottenhahn

This is delicious for cold winter evenings. We traditionally bake them for the 6th of December, Saint Nickolas Day!

Dough: (or your own creation)	
2¼ cups (250 gr) flour	1 egg
10 tablespoons (150 gr) butter	salt
⅓ cup (70 gr) sugar	1 teaspoon baking powder
	4-6 baking apples

Keep ingredients cool, mix quickly. Knead and roll with rolling pin into large square. Pare and core 4-6 medium sized baking apples and fill center with a mixture of ground almonds, raisins, sugar, cinnamon and butter. Cut dough into individual squares, large enough to enclose each apple. Brush dough with egg yolk. Set onto greased cookie sheet and bake in 350° oven for 30 minutes.

JOHANNISBEERLIKÖR AUS SCHLESWIG-HOLSTEIN
(Currant Liquor from Schleswig-Holstein)

Annelore Schmidt

1¼ cups (300 gr) currants	1 vanilla bean
¾ cup (150 gr) white sugar candy	1 bottle corn whiskey (38 proof)

Mix all ingredients together and keep in closed container. Shake occasionally. After 6-8 weeks remove berries and bean. Serve as a drink or over ice cream and puddings.

MARZIPAN PILZE
(Almond Paste Mushrooms)

Elisabeth Kottenhahn

Great grandmother Marx passed this recipe on to us.

Blanch 2 cups (9 oz. or 250 gr) almonds, let dry and grate finely. Mix with 1¼ cups (250 gr) sugar and 2 egg whites. Add grated chocolate to half of this mixture; leave the other half white. Form small balls out of both batters; use the darker one as head of the mushroom. Press a small hole into it and insert the lighter ball that has been shaped into a cone or something that looks like a mushroom stem. Let dry in the air. You might also wish to use these mushrooms to decorate the 'Baumstamm Kuchen'.

HERINGSSALAT
(Herring Salad)

Ursel Guy

In addition to baking the "Weihnachtsstollen" at Christmastime, I make a "Heringssalat" which my mother and my grandmother made. Since my grandmother died, my mother gives a small bowl full of this traditional salad to each of her brothers every Christmas because their wives have never made it. This salad is always welcome at my house; perhaps it's a nice change from the many cookies and sweets during the holidays.

- 2 salt herring (Clean and place in water for 2 hours. Change the water frequently. Sour herring can also be used).
- 1 large apple
- 1 large or 2 small celery stalks (cooked)
- 2 dill pickles
- 2 hard-boiled eggs
- 2 onions (cut very finely)
- ½ lb (227 gr) meat rests (I normally cook a big pot of soup or beef stock and use the meat for the salad
- ½ lb (227 gr) cooked beets
- 4 small potatoes (boiled with peel)
- 2-3 tablespoons mayonnaise
  vinegar and oil to taste
  salt and pepper to taste

Dice all ingredients and toss together in a bowl. Chill in refrigerator for 4 hours or overnight.

BUTTER Ss UND Qs
(Butter S's and Q's)

Pauline Zistl

- 4 cups (460 gr) flour (or a little less)
- 1 cup (227 gr) butter
- ¼ cup (50 gr) sugar
- 5 egg yolks
  grated lemon rind

On a wooden board mix all ingredients into a dough which is then chilled in refrigerator for ½ hour. Roll dough into ropes, about ⅓ inch in diameter, from which S's or Q's (little pretzels) are formed. Place these cookies on baking sheet and let stand over night in a cold place. Before baking, brush cookies with egg yolks or egg whites and dip in sugar or ground nuts. Bake at 350° for 12 minutes until golden brown.

LINZER TÖRTCHEN
(Linzer Cookies)

Lizzy Haenlein

Delicious cookies which should be baked the week of Christmas, not too early in December.

4 cups (2 lbs. or 950 gr) sugar
8 cups (2 lbs. or 950 gr) flour
8 cups (2 lbs. or 950 gr) almonds
1 teaspoon cloves
¼ cup (60 ml) Kirschwasser sprinkled into dough before rolling
1 egg yolk for glazing lattice on top
   strawberry jam for filling

2 lbs. (950 gr) butter
6-8 eggs
2 teaspoons cinnamon

Blend sugar and butter and mix until smooth. Gradually add other ingredients. Refrigerate until dough is cool (about 1 hour). Roll out onto a board and cut with a 3" cutter. Then cut half the cookies with a 1" cutter to form a hole in the center of the cookie. Completed cookie is like a sandwich with a hole in the top layer. Bake for 15-20 minutes at 350°F. After cookies are baked and cooled, dust the cookie with the hole with powdered sugar. Spread jam on the bottom layer and put the top layer on. Be careful that jam doesn't come out of sides.

SPITZBUBEN
(Little Rogues)

Pauline Zistl

These marmalade filled cookies are favorites of my family and guests each Christmas season (it must be the rogue in them!) They know what is good and everyone seems to eat up this cookie first.

½ cup (115 gr) butter
½ cup (100 gr) sugar
1⅔ cups (200 gr) flour
½ cup (65 gr) ground almonds

vanilla
2 cups (474 ml) marmalade
   raspberry, strawberry or family
favorite

Prepare dough by sifting flour onto a board or a large bowl. Cut butter into flour and blend all ingredients using a pastry blender, two knives or fingertips until the mixture sticks together and forms a ball. Chill. Roll out on floured board as thin as possible. Cut out rounds with a scalloped cookie cutter, about 2" in diameter and with a glass 1" smaller make a hole in the center of half the cookies, to form rings. Bake at 350° for 12-15 minutes until crisp and golden. Dust rings with sugar. Spread marmalade on bottom rounds and place ring on top.

HASELNUSSMAKRONEN
(Hazelnut Macaroons)

Lizzy Haenlein

12 egg whites (extra large)	3 tablespoons vanillin sugar
3¾ cups (750 gr) extra fine sugar	1 teaspoon vanilla extract
3 lbs. 4 oz. (1450 gr) ground hazelnuts	
(save enough whole nuts for each macaroon)	

Beat egg whites until stiff. Add sugar and beat at speed #4 for ½ hour. Add hazelnuts and flavoring by hand. Use a teaspoon and drop onto a rice wafer on parchment paper (on a cookie sheet). Set a whole hazelnut into the center of each macaroon. Bake immediately at 300° for 30-40 minutes. Bake only one sheet at a time and place baking rack on the bottom position of the oven for baking.
Makes 120 cookies.

These should be made at least three weeks before Christmas and placed in a tin to age. Layers of cookies should be divided with wax paper. Don't open!

KOKOSMAKRONEN
(Coconut Macaroons)

Elli Beck

4 egg whites	2¼ oz. (65 gr) low fat cottage cheese
¾ cup (150 gr) sugar	4 drops bitter almond extract
1 tablespoon vanilla extract	1¼ cups (200 gr) shredded coconut

Beat egg whites; add sugar and vanilla. Add cottage cheese, bitter almond extract and coconut. Combine gently. Drop by teaspoon onto a greased cookie sheet and bake 10-15 minutes at 350°F.

NÜSSLEIN
(Nut Cookies)

Martha Borbe

2 large egg whites	pinch of cream of tartar
2 cups (400 gr) light brown sugar	pinch of salt
3 cups (360 gr) pecans (or walnuts)	

Beat egg whites until stiff. Add cream of tartar, add light brown sugar gradually and thoroughly. Stir in nuts and salt. Place dough from a teaspoon onto a greased cookie sheet. Bake at 250° and then let cookies dry in oven for 1 hour. Store in a tin container.

ZIMTSTERNE
(Cinnamon Stars)

Lizzy Haenlein

16 egg whites
2 lbs. (950 gr) powdered sugar
4 lbs. (1800 gr) ground almonds

1 lb. (454 gr) ground hazelnuts
1 oz. cinnamon

Beat egg whites until stiff. Add sugar and beat one hour at #4 speed. Remove 4 tablespoons for icing. To remainder add with a wooden spoon the nuts and cinnamon. Roll out small amounts on ground almonds and cut with small star cutter. Do not roll too thin. Place on parchment paper, brush with egg white icing and let stand in cool place for 4 hours. Bake for 30 minutes at 275°F. Bake only one sheet at a time and place rack on bottom oven position. Clean cutter thoroughly after each cutting.

Makes about 150 cookies.
These cookies taste best when made 3 weeks ahead of time and stored in a tin in a cool place.

ZITRONEN HERZEN
(Lemon Hearts)

Lizzy Haenlein

This recipe yields about 50 cookies. If you wish a larger quantity, use the underlined ingredients in parentheses for a yield of approximately 200 cookies.

3 egg yolks (12 yolks)
⅔ cup (120 gr) sugar (1 lb. 2 oz.)
1 package vanillin sugar - (available at gourmet shops) or 1 tablespoon vanilla (4 packages vanillin sugar) or (4 tablespoons vanilla)
3 drops lemon extract (1 teaspoon)
1 pinch baking powder (⅛ teaspoon)
7-9 oz. (200-250 gr) almonds (2 lbs. 4 oz.) (blanched and ground)

Beat warm yolks until thick and light colored. Add the sugars and beat well. Add lemon extract and baking powder. Add almonds until thick and finish adding by hand. Knead in enough so dough does not stick on sides. Roll the dough on almonds or confectionery sugar. Use a heart cutter and cut out thin cookies. Lay on parchment paper and bake at 375°F. for 10 minutes. Ice as soon as you remove from sheet.

Icing:
⅔ cup (100 gr) confectioner sugar
1-1½ teaspoons lemon juice

BUTTERGEBÄCK

(Butter Cookies)

Lizzy Haenlein

3 sticks (340 gr) butter
1 cup (7 oz.) sugar
7 egg yolks

4½ cups (500 gr) sifted flour
3 teaspoons vanilla

Beat yolks and sugar ½ hour at #4 speed. Add vanilla, soft butter and flour. Roll in loaf and place in refrigerator to cool for rolling. Use design cutters and brush each cut out with egg yolk. Roll only sufficient dough which can be handled without getting too warm. Decorate with sprinkles, etc. and bake on middle rack in oven for 8-10 minutes at 350°F. Since these can burn easily, be careful to check frequently.

BUTTERPLÄTZCHEN

(Butter Cookies)

Trudy Rueggeberg

2 cups (454 gr) butter
2¼ cups (450 gr) sugar
4 eggs

5½ cups (630 gr) sifted flour
salt
lemon rind

Let butter stand at room temperature until soft. Cream in large mixer bowl for 1 minute (speed #8). Gradually add sugar at same speed and beat for another minute. Scrape bowl often. Add unbeaten eggs one at a time. Reduce mixer to speed #1. Add flour, salt and lemon rind. Mix until well blended. Roll out ⅛ inch thick. Bake at 350° for 10-12 min. on a greased cookie sheet.

SPITZE PLÄTZCHEN

(Lace Cookies)

Roberta A. Mayer

My grandfather's lace cookie recipe — one of my favorites!

Preheat oven to 325°F.

1 lb. (454 gr) brown sugar
10 tablespoons (5 oz. or 150 gr) butter
¼ cup (2 oz. or 60 ml) honey
½ cup (125 ml) water

10 oz. (280 gr) walnuts—coarsely chopped
2 cups (230 gr) flour
dash of salt
1 teaspoon cinnamon

Melt butter in a double boiler. Add sugar, honey, and water. Bring to boil over medium heat. Remove from heat and blend in remaining ingredients. When dough is uniform in consistancy, drop by teaspoons onto a well-greased baking sheet. Bake until set, about 8 to 10 minutes. Quickly remove from baking sheet and let cool on racks. Melt 12 oz. of semi-sweet chocolate chips in double boiler. Spread melted chocolate over the smooth side of the cooled cookies. Let chocolate harden. Store cookies in air-tight containers.

SPRITZ SPEZIALITÄTEN
(Spritz Specials)

Dorothy Dodds

Cookies are very special at Christmas time and my mother makes about 30 different kinds. This is one of the most popular and a favorite of family and friends. I enjoy making these too!

Using the bar cookie insert in the cookie press, form 1½-2 inch long bars.
Dough:
1 lb. (2 cups or 454 gr) butter
1½ cups (300 gr) sugar
4-5 cups (460-575 gr) flour

2 eggs
2 teaspoons vanilla

Bake at 375° for 10-12 minutes. When cookies have cooled, spread seedless raspberry jam between 2 cookies, making a "Sandwich". Dip both ends of sandwich in chocolate mixture composed of:

12 oz. (336 gr) semi-sweet chocolate ⎫
2-3 walnut-sized pieces of paraffin ⎭   melted over hot water

and immediately into finely chopped pecans.

SPRITZGEBÄCK
(Spritz Cookies)

Maria Lacquer

3 sticks or 1½ cups (340 gr) butter
1 cup (200 gr) sugar
1 egg
1 teaspoon vanilla extract

½ teaspoon almond extract
4 cups (460 gr) sifted flour
1 teaspoon baking powder

Cream butter and sugar. Add egg, vanilla and almond extract; mix well. Sift flour with the baking powder and add little by little and mix until batter becomes smooth. Do not cool in refrigerator! Squeeze dough through cookie press onto an ungreased cookie sheet. Bake in hot (400°) oven about 8 minutes. Let cool.
Makes about 6 dozen. Cookies can be decorated with chocolate glaze.

Glaze:
1½ oz. (42 gr) unsweetened chocolate
2 tablespoons butter

1½ cups (200 gr) sifted powdered sugar
1 teaspoon vanilla extract

Melt chocolate and butter over low heat, stirring continuously. Remove from flame and add sugar and vanilla; mix well. Add 2-3 tablespoons boiling water. Dip ends of Spritz cookies into glaze, dry on waxed paper, or spread glaze over cookies.

SPRITZGEBACKENES
(Cookies From the Press)

Gudrun McGee

3¼ cups (375 gr) flour

1 cup + 2 tablespoons (250 gr) butter
1⅓ cups (180 gr) sugar
1 package vanillin sugar (available at gourmet shops) or 1 teaspoon vanilla
4.5 oz. (125 gr) blanched-ground almonds
2 eggs

Cut the butter into small pieces and mix with the sugar, eggs and almonds. Stir in the flour to form the cookie dough. Using a cookie-press form small S-shaped cookies and place them onto a well-greased cookie sheet. Bake at 350° for approximately 30 minutes.

SPRITZGEBÄCK
(Cookie Press Cookies)

Ruth Olivier

This is a recipe for very fattening and delicious cookies. My mother made them all the time and I have experimented with the measurement conversion. My family also considers these a favorite and they enjoy them especially at Christmas.

½ lb. (227 gr) sweet whipped butter
1 cup (200 gr) sugar
1 egg

1 package (3½ oz.) ground Brazil or hazelnuts
2½ cups (250 gr) sifted flour

Cream butter and sugar, add the rest of the ingredients and work into a fluffy dough. Let the dough rest several hours or overnight and press rings, question marks or anything your heart desires (with a spritz cookie press gun) on a cookie sheet, dusted with flour. Bake at 325° for 15 - 20 minutes. I watch them like a hawk, because they should be a golden color, so I take some out, turn others around. Since they don't seem to bake evenly, I leave some in longer.

SPRINGERLE
(Springerle)

Leni Holzhauser

4 eggs
4 cups (454 gr) flour
2¼ cups (454 gr) sugar

anise oil, 4 drops
anise seed for pan

Beat whole eggs until thick. Add sugar gradually, beating well between each addition until all is combined; then beat well for aobut 15 minutes. This makes the finished cookies fine grained and light. Add the anise oil and blend. Fold in the flour lightly. Roll out the dough about ½ inch thick. Flour the Springerle mold carefully and press firmly into dough. Remove mold and cut the cookies along the line of the imprint. Place on buttered cookie sheets. Flour the mold each time it is used. Sprinkle anise seed if desired on the buttered cookie sheets before placing the cookies on them. Let cookies stand overnight in a cool place to dry. In the morning place in a moderate oven (350°) to set the shape but reduce to 325° after 5 minutes. In 15 minutes the cookies should be light in color with the appearance of having been iced.

SPRINGERLE
(Springerle)

Elisabeth Kottenhahn

A foolproof recipe from grandmother Andreas!

2 eggs	grated rind of half a lemon
2 cups (250 gr) confectioners	2¼ cups (250 gr) flour
sugar (or fine sugar)	1 teaspoon baking powder

Beat egg whites until stiff, but not dry. Add sugar and egg yolks and stir for 45 minutes - with an electric beater mix for approximately 15 minutes. Add lemon rind, sifted flour and baking powder. Knead dough until soft and smooth. Let stand in cool place for 1 hour. Roll out dough to ¼ inch thickness. Press with floured cookie mold. Cut out cookies with sharp knife or wheel cutter. Set cookies on greased cookie sheet sprinkled with anise. Let dry in cool (not cold) room overnight. Bake carefully in moderate oven until golden on the bottom and white on top.

SPRINGERLE
(Springerle)

Ida Stein

4 cups (454 gr) flour, sifted	1 tablespoon butter
2¼ cups (454 gr) sugar	1 teaspoon baking powder
4 large eggs	¾ cup anise seeds

Beat sugar, butter, eggs, and baking powder (dissolved in small amount of milk) together for 15 minutes. Add flour gradually until dough thickens. Place dough on floured board, knead until shiny. With a rolling pin roll out to ½ inch thickness. Flour a springerle board or form and press or roll design over dough. Cut pieces apart and place on a baking sheet (or board) that is sprinkled with anise seeds. Let dry overnight (or 24 hrs.) at room temperature. Butter a baking sheet, place springerle on it and bake in 250° oven until pale white about 15 - 20 minutes.

NÜRNBERGER ELISEN-LEBKUCHEN
(Spice Cakes)

Elli Beck

5 egg whites	1 teaspoon orange rind
2¼ cups (450 gr) sugar	1 teaspoon lemon rind
1 teaspoon cinnamon	4 oz. (112 gr) each, lemon and
1 teaspoon cloves, ground	orange peel, ground up
1 teaspoon cornstarch	1 lb. (454 gr) ground hazelnuts

Beat egg whites with sugar, add above ingredients. Spread dough on communion wafers (Oblaten), decorate with almonds. Bake at 325°F. about 15 minutes. Cool completely and brush on glaze.

Glaze: 1¾ cups (230 gr) confectioners sugar; mix with 3-4 tablespoons rum or lemon juice.

LEBKUCHEN
(Honey Spice Cakes)

Elly Gilgenast

What would Christmas have been without the "Bunter Teller" Everyone in the family would get a special plate under the Christmas tree filled with goodies, such as apples, nuts, candy, and all kinds of cookies. Here is one of the favorite cookie recipes that appeared on the plate:

½ cup (120 ml) honey
½ cup (120 ml) molasses   mix and bring to boil, cool thoroughly

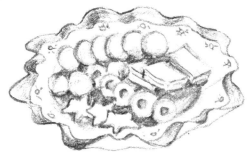

stir in
¾ cup (150 gr) brown sugar, packed
1 egg
1 tablespoon lemon juice
1 teaspoon grated lemon rind

sift together and stir in
2¾ cups (230 gr) sifted flour
½ teaspoon baking soda
1 teaspoon cinnamon
1 teaspoon cloves
1 teaspoon allspice
1 teaspoon nutmeg

mix in
⅓ cup (80 ml) cut up citron
⅓ cup (80 ml) chopped nuts

Chill dough overnight. Roll small amount at a time, keeping rest chilled. Roll out ¼ inch thick and cut into oblongs 1½ x 2½. Place 1 inch apart on greased baking sheet. Bake until no imprint remains when touched lightly. While cookies bake, make Glaze Icing. Brush it over cookies the minute they are out of the oven. Then quickly remove from baking sheet, cool and store to mellow. Temp. 350° mod. hot, 10 - 12 min.

Glaze Icing: Boil together 1 cup (200 gr) sugar and ½ cup (120 ml) water until first indication of a thread appears (230°). Remove from heat. Stir in ¼ cup confectioners sugar and brush hot icing thinly over cookies. (When icing gets sugary, reheat slightly, adding a little water until clear again).

CHRISTMAS STOLLEN
Johanna M. Hilsenrad

Sometimes a special recipe brings memories of a special time or a special place in your life. So it is with the recipe for *Christmas-Stollen* and together with the recipe I would like to share the memories with you.

Saxony, in the southeastern section of Germany, is where I was born. I spent my childhood in Chemnitz, known today as Karl-Marx-Stadt. It was then and still is today a large industrial center, situated in the foothills of the Erzgebirge, or Ore Mountains, a mountain range dividing Germany and Czechoslovakia. It was a silver mining center, but more important and sheer magic for children, it was the cottage-industry center for the manufacture of toys and Christmas tree decorations, which were sent to all the world.

Perhaps that's why the pre-Christmas season was so special for us children at home. Advent! At night by candlelight and goodies to eat, we shared stories which were read and sang and played music together. The children, there were four of us, were allowed to stay up longer than usual, and the special preparations for the holiday baking season began. First the cookies! My mother rolled out the dough and we children cut out all the fancy forms that were later to hang on our tree. Then the Stollen! The special recipes native to the area and jealously guarded by each family which has its own variations, are sometimes known as *Dresdner Christstollen*, after the capitol of Saxony; however, it originated right in the region where I grew up. They were a family affair. We children would blanch and peel sweet and bitter almonds and clean and pick over raisins of three different varieties. Each of us watched closely that not too much was detoured into the other three mouths. We watched and learned as the grownups cut citron and prepared all the other ingredients for this once a year delicacy, the traditional Weihnachtsstollen!

Now I have lived in the U.S. for thirty years, but I still keep house the way I learned to do so long ago at home, and the special customs have never lost their meanings. My daughter and her family celebrate Advent and Christmas in much the same way, having learned in my house when she was little, and I hope that someday my only granddaughter will continue and carry on the customs and bakery of this loveliest time of the year.

WEIHNACHTSSTOLLEN

Johanna M. Hilsenrad

deutsche Pfunde

2 Pf. Mehl	100 g süsse Mandeln
½ Pf. Butter	16 g bittere Mandeln
150 g Zucker	70 g Hefe
250 g Rosinen	¼-½ 1 Milch
250 g Korinthen	etwas Salz
50 g Zitronat	Schale einer geriebenen zitrone

In eine tiefe Schüssel gibt man das Mehl und füllt in die Mitte die mit lauwarmer Milch aufgelöste Hefe und eine kleine Prise Zucker und stellt es zum Gehen. Vorher wird die Butter aufgelöst und zu Milch und Hefe getan. Dann knetet man diesen Teig durch und fügt die anderen Zutaten nach und nach dazu. Der Teig wird noch einmal an eine warme Stelle gestellt (1 Stunde) und dann rollt man das Ganze auf einem vorgewärmten Brett aus, klappt den Teig um und backt den Stollen bei guter Hitze eine Stunde, bestreicht ihn dann mit viel Butter und Zucker. Die Butter zum Bestreichen muss zerlassen sein und warm.

WEIHNACHTSSTOLLEN
(Christmas Stollen)

8 cups (1 kilo) flour	3.5 oz. (100 gr) sweet almonds
½ lb. (227 gr) butter	.5 oz. (16 gr) bitter almonds
¾ cup (150 gr) sugar	2 packages dry yeast
9 oz. (250 gr) raisins	1-2 cups (¼-½ liter) milk
9 oz. (250 gr) currants	some salt
2 oz. (50 gr) citron	grated rind of 1 lemon

In a deep bowl put flour and form a well. Place into center the yeast which has been dissolved in lukewarm milk with a little sugar added. Melt the butter and add to milk and yeast. Let this rise in a warm place. Then knead this dough thoroughly and gradually add the other ingredients. Place the dough again in a warm place for about 1 hour and let it rise. Then roll the dough out on a pre-warmed board, fold the dough over, form into 4 large loaves and bake in a 350° oven about ½ to 1 hour. When finished, brush the top with warm melted butter and dust with powdered sugar.

WEIHNACHTSSTOLLEN
(Christmas Stollen)

Erika Glaeser

Each period and each region in Germany has brought forth its own Christmas specialties. From Dresden comes the **Christmas-Stollen.** At the beginning of Advent the Dresden Hausfrau starts with the baking of the Stollen from an old family recipe. The Stollen is well wrapped and stored until Christmas. Only then is it served for the first time at a festive coffee table by the glow of the candle lit tree.

In the Middle Ages the Christmas-Stollen would not be eaten before the 28th of December, the day the innocent children were slaughtered in Bethlehem. The shape of the Stollen with its white coating symbolizes the little children wrapped in white cloth.

This has always been a favorite in my husband's family and among our guests. I begin to bake these in November and put them into the freezer. I have found they keep well and actually get better and moister.

6 cups (700 gr) all purpose flour	¼ lb. (113 gr) blanched, chopped almonds
1½-2 cakes yeast	½ cup (120 ml) citron
¾ cup (150 gr) sugar	nutmeg
10 oz. (280 gr) butter	salt
1 lb. (454 gr) raisins	1 lemon (grated lemon peel and juice)
(dark or blanched or mixed)	⅔ cup milk

All ingredients should be warm, about 75°. Sift flour into large bowl Make an indentation in the middle of the flour, crumble yeast cake into it, add some of the sugar and 3 tablespoons warmed milk. Stir a little of the flour into it with a wooden spoon to make a soft dough ball. Cover the bowl and let the dough rise about 30 minutes (kitchen must be warm and free of drafts).
Next Step: Sprinkle rest of sugar over flour and into the dough ball, adding rest of the milk until the dough is firm and pulls away from the bowl.
Next Step: Mix fruits and spices and lemon juice. Work into dough. Then form large oval or two smaller loaves, fold in half lengthwise or ⅔ to ⅓ and put on greased cookie sheet. Let rise for one hour, covered. Bake at 350° for 50 minutes.

WEIHNACHTSSTOLLEN
(Christmas Stollen)

Elly Gilgenast

10 cups (1.2 kilo) flour	4 oz. (113 gr) citron
1 lb. (454 gr) butter	1 teaspoon salt
2 cups (474 ml) milk	½ teaspoon cardamon
1 cup (200 gr) sugar	½ teaspoon nutmeg
3 eggs	3 packages dry yeast

1⅔ cups (227 gr) white raisins ⎫
1⅔ cups (227 gr) currants ⎬ soak several hours in rum
1 cup (113 gr) blanched, chopped almonds ⎭

Dissolve yeast in ½ cup lukewarm milk with a little sugar. Let it rise. Cream butter, add eggs and sugar and all spices. To flour add yeast and then add butter/spice mixture. Knead lightly to make a soft dough. Place in large bowl, cover with thin towel and set in warm place free from draft. Let rise for several hours until doubled in bulk. Shape into 4 equal size stollen and bake about 30-40 minutes at 350°. While still hot after baking, brush with melted butter or margarine and dust with powdered sugar.

WEIHNACHTSSTOLLEN
(Christmas Stollen)

Heidi Valiente

1 cup (237 ml) milk
½ cup (100 gr) granulated sugar
½ teaspoon salt
1 package active dry yeast
¼ cup (60 ml) warm, not hot water
1 cup (115 gr) sifted all-purpose flour
½ cup (120 ml) finely cut candied cherries
½ cup (120 ml) finely cut citron
1 cup (112 gr) slivered, blanched almonds
grated rind 1 lemon
1 cup (170 gr) raisins
2 eggs, well beaten

¾ cup (170 gr) soft butter or margarine
¼ teaspoon nutmeg
3 cups (345 gr) sifted all-purpose flour
1 cup (115 gr) sifted all-purpose flour
¼ cup (60 gr) melted butter or margarine
½ teaspoon cinnamon
2 tablespoons granulated sugar

Early in day: In very large saucepan, scald milk, add ½ cup sugar and salt, cool till lukewarm. Meanwhile, sprinkle yeast onto warm water. When milk is lukewarm, stir in yeast and 1 cup flour. Use egg beater to remove any lumps. Now cover dough, set in warm place (about 85°F) to rise until double in bulk - about 2 hours.
While waiting for dough to rise, prepare all fruits and nuts. When dough has risen, stir in citron, cherries, almonds, lemon rind, raisins, eggs, soft butter, nutmeg. Stir in 3 cups flour.
On lightly floured surface, knead 1 cup flour into dough until dough is smooth and elastic. Roll into large 18 x 12 inch oval, about ½ inch thick. Brush with melted butter, sprinkle with combined cinnamon and 2 tablespoons sugar.
Make lengthwise crease down center of dough, fold over. Remove to large greased baking sheet. Push into shape of crescent, then, with palm of hand press down along crease to shape. Brush with melted butter. Cover with waxed paper, then with clean towel, set in warm place to rise till nearly double in bulk.
Start heating oven to 350°F. Then bake 30 to 40 min., or until golden. Sprinkle cooled Stollen with sifted confectioners' sugar. Keeps well.

WEIHNACHTSSTOLLEN
(Christmas Stollen)

Elli Beck

24 cups (2.7 kilo) flour	4 oz. (113 gr) lemon peel ⎫
2¼ cups (400 gr) sugar	4 oz. (113 gr) orange peel ⎬ candied
1 lb. (454 gr) butter	4 oz. (113 gr) citrus peel ⎭
1 cup (227 gr) lard	3 cups (700 ml) milk
4 cups (680 gr) raisins	8 oz. (227 gr) slivered almonds
5 eggs	6 packages dried yeast
1 rind of lemon	
1 teaspoon almond flavoring	

Make dough, add all fruits and nuts, let rise about 1½ hours. Then form into 4 or 5 Stollen; let rise again. Bake at 350° about 1 hour, brush with melted butter then sprinkle with powdered sugar.

WEIHNACHTSSTOLLEN
(Christmas Stollen)

Luise Evers

12 cups (1.4 kilo) flour
3 lbs. (1.4 kilo) raisins-½ dark, ½ white (not muscatels)

4 fresh yeast cakes	
2¼ cups (454 gr) sugar	6 eggs
2 teaspoons salt	2 lbs. (950 gr) butter
1 lb. (454 gr) citron-chopped fine	¾ lbs. (335 gr) almonds
about 3 cups (700 ml) lukewarm milk	½ teaspoon cardamon

The night before you make the dough sprinkle rum over raisins, then next morning sprinkle some flour and mix with raisins.
Mix 1 cup flour, milk and yeast - let rise. While this yeast mixture is rising, cream sugar, butter and eggs. Then add the yeast mixture and remaining flour and beat well with hands. Let rise until double in size. Then push down the dough and add citron, raisins, almonds and cardamon, mix well. Shape into three stollen and let the loaves rise until double in size. Bake for 10 minutes at 375° - then 15 or 20 minutes at 325°. After baking, cool a little then dribble butter over stollen and sprinkle with sugar - cinnamon optional.

WEIHNACHTSSTOLLEN
(Gramma's Famous Stollen - Christmas or Easter)

Lisa Weinauer

2 cakes or envelopes yeast
1¾ cups (420 ml) milk,
    (scalded and cooled)
7½ cups (850 gr) regular flour
½ cup (100 gr) sugar

2 eggs
grated rind of 1 lemon
2 teaspoons salt
½ cup (113 gr) shortening - butter
or oleo
1-4 oz. (113 gr) package chopped citron
1-4 oz. (113 gr) package candied lemon
peel
1-4 oz. (113 gr) package orange peel
1 cup (237 ml) raisins
¾ cup (180 ml) chopped almonds

Dissolve yeast as suggested on package, slowly add the liquid which has
been cooled to 80°F. Sift flour once before measuring. Add the sugar, beaten
eggs, salt and flour to the first mixture, add the softened shortening and
mix thoroughly with hands, about 15 min. until smooth (knead gently).
Place in well greased bowl, cover and let rise until dough has doubled its
bulk - at 80° (about 1½ hours). Punch dough down and let rise 30 min. or
until ¾ its bulk. Roll out slightly and place fruit mixture and almonds in
center, fold over and knead until evenly distributed. Divide into two loaves,
then round up on board and let stand 15 minutes. Roll out slightly, forming
long ovals and spread top with melted butter. Press down center and fold
over each loaf like a pocketbook. Brush again with butter. Let rise about 1
hour until double its bulk and bake at 375°F for 40 minutes. When taken
from oven, brush with confectioner's sugar as icing. Bake at least one week
ahead of time - keeps well and freezes well too.

Guten Appetit

FRÜCHTEBROT
(Fruit Bread)

Vera Schock

A favorite holiday treat in our family is this bread which is similar to fruit
cake.

3 eggs
¾ cup (150 gr) sugar
1 teaspoon vanilla extract
3 teaspoons
imitation rum extract
½ teaspoon cinnamon

1 cup (115 gr) sifted all-purpose flour
1 teaspoon baking powder
1⅓ cups (300 ml) chopped nuts
¾ cup (180 ml) chopped candied
citrus fruits
¾ cup (180 ml) golden seedless
raisins .

Sift together flour and baking powder. Beat eggs; beat in sugar gradually.
Add vanilla, rum and cinnamon. Stir in sifted dry ingredients. Beat for one
minute. Stir in nuts and fruits. Mix well. Pour into a greased and floured loaf
pan. Bake in slow oven (325°) for 45 minutes to one hour or until done. Let
cool for ½ hour before removing from pan.

KNUSPERHÄUSCHEN
(Gingerbread House)

Lizzy Haenlein

The entire family has fun in baking and building this house. Each year we have had a uniquely creative Hänsel and Gretel house. One can do what one wishes: make shutters of almonds, icicles of running icing, a gumdrop tree, hard candy and candy canes to decorate. It has become a tradition that everyone eats the 'Knusperhäuschen' on New Year's Eve!

⅔ cup (130 gr) brown sugar
½ cup (120 ml) molasses
2 teaspoons ginger
1 teaspoon cloves
4 teaspoons cinnamon

⅔ cup (7 oz. or 200 gr) butter
1 egg
2 teaspoons baking soda
4 cups (460 gr) flour

Cook up sugar, molasses and spices. Add baking soda and stir until it is frothy. Add butter and stir until it melts. Add egg. When all is cool, add flour a little at a time. Knead on baking board and roll out not too thick (¼ inch) on lightly floured board. Form pieces of house (see diagram which follows) on cookie sheet and bake for 6-8 minutes at 350°F. Make icing from powdered sugar and water and use a fairly thick consistency to put house together. I use icing in a pastry bag. Build up house on a lazy susan beginning with sides and dormers, then the roof and chimney. First prepare a floor of hard candy which helps to support the sides. After the sides are up, wait 2 hours and then put on the roof and chimney. Decorate the rest of the house to your heart's desire!

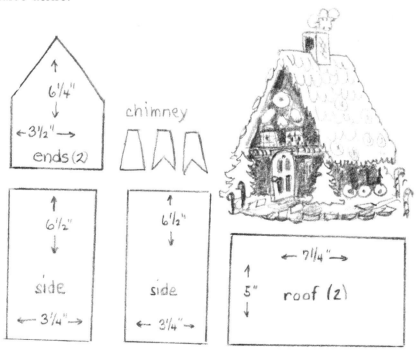

156

ZWETSCHGEN MANDERLN
(Prune People)

Hilde Cox

As seen at the Nürnberger Christkindlesmarkt!

Material:
½ inch disc of a small birch log
1 coat hanger
12 prunes
4 figs
1 walnut, 2 small almonds
scraps of fabric

The origin of these prune people is unknown; however, they may have been made as gifts for children to be eaten at Christmas time.

1. Cut a coat hanger 4 inches in length from the neck; cut off the top. Bend into two long straight legs.

2. Push each leg through three prunes the long way; the fourth prune the short way to form the shoe. Secure the two legs in the holes drilled into the wooden disc.

3. Push three or four figs over the neck of the coat hanger.

4. Use an 8 inch piece of the coat hanger for the arms. Push it through the fig on top; add two prunes on either side and finish with a small almond as a hand.

5. Glue a walnut on top of the wire extending from the figs.

Use your imagination and decorate the prune doll into anything or anybody you want! They can wear dirndls and lederhosen; they can be backpackers or motorcyclists, pair off as bride or bridegroom, butcher or baker, chimney sweep or vegetable lady! Have fun!

SOURCES OF INFORMATION

Carlton, Mike, *"Fasching!"* THE PHILADELPHIA INQUIRER, February 9, 1975.

Hayes, Colleen, *"You haven't lived it up till you live up an Oktoberfest"*. THE PHILADELPHIA INQUIRER, September 30, 1979.

Hole, Christina, *Christmas and its customs*. New York, 1958.

Kramer, Dieter, *German Holidays and Folk Customs*. ATLANTIKBRÜCKE, Hamburg, 1972.

Ruland, Josef, *Christmas in Germany*. HOHWACHT, Bonn, 1978.

INDEX
Holiday - German titles

SILVESTER UND NEUJAHR (New Year's Eve and New Year)

Bayrische Knödel *Potato Dumplings* 23
Beefsteak Tartar *Beefsteak Tartar* 17
Eierlikor *Eggnog* 15
Feuerzangenbowle *Firetong or rum punch* 14
Fleischsalat *Cooked meat salad* 18
Glückliche Fliegenpilz-Männer *Good luck mushroom men* 20
Glühwein *Spiced wine* 15
Gotterspeise *A dish pleasing to the gods* 25
Grüne Klösse *Raw potato dumplings* 24
Gurkenschiffchen *Cucumber boats* 21
Heringssalat *Herring salad* 17
Husaren Punsch *Elite artillery punch* 15
Kalte Platte *Cold - cut platter* 18
Kartoffelsalat *Potato salad* 16
Käse Stiks *Assorted cheese appetizers* 19
Linsensuppe *Lentil soup* 22
Muttis Berliner Pfannekuchen *Mother's Berliner donuts* 24
Pikante Zungenschnitten *Tasty sliced tongue* 18
Punsch für Kalte Abende (in German and English) *Punch for cold evenings* 16
Rostbraten *Steak* 22
Rote Rüben Eier *Red-beet eggs* 20
Russische Eier *Russian eggs* 20
Saure Linsen mit Spätzle *Sour lentils with noodles* 21
Schinken-Hawaii *Ham toast - Hawaii style* 19
Seidenklösse *Dumplings* 23
Tartarbrötchen *Tartar* 17
Wurstsalat *Wurst salad* 19

FASCHING (Carnival, Mardi Gras, Fasching)

Bayerische Brotknödel *Bavarian bread dumplings* 38
Berliner Krapfen - Faschingskrapfen *Jelly Doughnuts* 28
Brotknödel *Bread dumplings* 38
Dampfnudeln (in German and English) *Steamed sweet dumplings* 34, 35, 36
Eierkuchen *Pancakes* 29
Eiernockerl *Egg dumplings* 31
Fastnachts *Doughnuts* 28
Flädlesuppe *Soup with pancake strips* 39
Griessnockerlsuppe *Farina or cream of wheat soup* 38
Kaiserschmarren *Emperor's pancakes* 30
Kartoffelpuffer *Potato pancakes* 37
Kirschenjokel *Cherry souffle* 31
Krapfen *Raisin doughnuts* 29
Maultaschen *Mouth pockets or filled noodles* 32
Pfannkuchensuppe *Pancake soup* 39
Pflaumenknödel aus Topfenteig *Cottage cheese plum dumplings* 33
Scheiterhaufen (in German and English) *Swabian lenten dish* 30
Vanilla Sauce *Vanilla sauce* 33

OSTERN (Easter)

Bauernfrühstück *Farmer's breakfast* 45
Baumkuchen *Tree cake* 50

Brötchen *Rolls* 46
Forelle blau *Blue trout* 44
Frankfurter Kranz *Frankfurt wreath* 51
Gefüllter Kranz *Coffee ring* 50
Grüne Sosse *Green sauce* 43
Hefeklösse *Yeast dumplings* 44
Hefezopf *Yeast braid* 46
Nusstorte *Nut torte* 49
Osterbrezen *Easter pretzels* 46
Osterkrone *Easter bread* 45
Osterlammkuchen *Easter lamb cake* 47
Prophetenkuchen *Cake of the prophets* 50
Speckkuchen *Bacon cake* 43
Spinat und Spiegelei *Spinach and eggs* 43
Zimt Hefe Schnecken *Cinnamon buns* 48
Zimt Nusskuchen *Cinnamon nut coffee cake* 49

HIMMELFAHRT, PFINGSTEN, TAG DER ARBEIT
(Ascension, Pentecost, Labor Day and Hot Summer Days)

Bayrischer Krautsalat *Bavarian cabbage salad* 56
Berliner Kalbsleber *Fried calves liver* 63
Berliner Leber *Fried liver with onions and apples* 63
Biskuitteig zu Törtchen oder Obstkuchen *Fruit tarts* 72
Blaubeeren Kuchen *Blueberry cake* 73
Erdbeerblitz Torte *Strawberry Blitz Torte* 69
Gefüllte Krautwickel *Stuffed cabbage rolls* 60
Grießschmarren *Farina pudding* 81
Himmel und Erde *Heaven and earth* 64
Hühner Frikassee *Chicken fricassee* 62
Hühner oder Kalbsfrikassee *Chicken or veal fricassee* 61
Kalbsfrikassee *Veal fricassee* 62
Kartoffelsalat *Potato salad* 56
Kirschenmichel mit Schwarzbrot *Cherry cake with rye bread* 72
Kirschkuchen mit Griess *Cherry cake with farina* 73
Kirschtorte *Cherry torte* 72
Klopse mit Saurer Sahne *German meatballs with sour cream* 66
Königsberger Klopse *Meatballs in caper sauce* 64, 65, 66
Kopfsalat (in German and English) Boston lettuce 70, 71
Kraut Strudel *Cabbage strudel* 60
Labskaus (in German and English) Sailor's hash 67, 68
Labskaus a la Helga (in German and English) Helga's hash 67, 68
Leberknödel *Liver dumplings* 64
Leipziger Allerlei *Mixed vegetables a la Leipzig* 59
Maultaschen *Meat filled noodles* 61
Paradieskraut *Paradise cabbage* 55
Pfirsich Bowle *Peach punch* 82
Pickelsteiner *Stew* 69
Prinkenauer Salat *Prinkenauer potato salad* 57
Quarkkuchen *Cottage cheese cake* 76
Quarktorte *Cottage cheese torte* 77
Rhabarberauflauf *Rhubarb souffle* 80
Rhabarberkompott *Stewed rhubarb* 81
Rhabarbertorte *Rhubarb pie* 74
Rheinische Sauce *Rhine sauce* 55
Rote Grütze *Red fruit pudding* 80
Rotkraut *Red cabbage* 58
Rührkuchen *Basic cake with fruit topping* 73

Rumtopf *Rum and fruit crock* 81
Saure Kirschen Suppe *Sour cherry soup* 58
Schinkenhörnchen *Ham filled pockets* 62
Schinkennudeln (in German and English) *Ham noodle souffle* 70, 71
Selleriesalat *Celeriac salad* 56
Selleriescheiben *hot celeriac* 56
Siebenlöffel Sauce *Seven spoon sauce* 55
Schnüsch *Vegetable chowder* 59
Spargel Suppe *Asparagus Soup* 57
Spargel Toast Daniel *Asparagus Toast Daniel* 57
Streusel *Crumbs* 75
Suss-Sauer Kraut *Sweet-sour cabbage* 55
Süss-Saure Sosse für Salat *Sweet-sour sauce for salad* 55
Tortenboden *Sponge cake for torte* 75
Vanillecreme (in German and English) *Vanilla creme* 78
Vanillesosse *Vannila sauce* 78
Weincreme *Wine creme* 78
Weinsosse *Wine sauce* 79
Zitronencreme *Lemon creme* 79
Zwetschendatschi *Plum tart* 74
Zwetschgenkuchen *Plum cake on a sheet* 75
Zwetschgenröster *Rum laced stewed plums* 80

HERBST FESTE *(Autumn)*

Amerikaner *Old fashioned German vanilla cookies* 108
Angemachter Camembert *Camembert spread* 107
Apfelkuchen (in German and English) *Applecake* 110, 111, 112, 113
Apfelkuchen mit Streuseln *Apple cake with crumb topping* 114
Apfelscheiben in Eierteig *Dessert apple fritters* 115
Apfelstrudel *Apple strudel* 114
Backobst und Klösse *Dried fruit and dumplings* 103
Berliner Schusterjungen Salzkuchen *Shoemaker's apprentices salt rolls* 88
Bratkartoffeln *Home fries* 106
Eintopf *Pot pie* 96
Erbsensuppe *Split pea soup* 90
Erbsensuppe mit Knackwurst *Split pea soup with knockwurst* 90
Feine Àpfelschnitten *Applecake* 112
Frische Suppe mit Klössen *Fresh soup with dumplings* 91
Gefülltes Meterbrot *Sausage loaf* 106
Grosser Hans *Steamed pudding* 107
Gulyassuppe *Goulash soup* 92
Gurken mit Fleischfüllung *Stuffed cucumbers* 106
Hasenpfeffer *Rabbit stew* 96
Hausgemachte Bratwurst *Homemade sausage* 107
Hobelspäne oder Räderkuchen *Woodshavings or wheel cakes* 109
Igel *Hedge hog* 109
Jägerschnitzel *Hunter's veal cutlet* 97
Kalter Hund-Die Echte Palmin-Kekstorte *Cold dog cookie torte* 109
Kaninchenbraten *Roasted tame rabbit* 96
Kartoffelklösse *Potato dumplings* 102
Kartoffelsuppe *Potato soup* 89, 90
Käse Blitzen *Quick cheese appetizers* 88
Kasseler Rippespeer *Pork loin* 99
Krautsuppe *Cabbage soup* 89
Leberkäse *Hot liver pate* 92
Lebernockerlsuppe *Liver dumpling soup* 88
Markklösschensuppe *Marrow dumpling soup* 89

Mehlbeutel *Dumplings* 104
Original Ditmarscher Mehlbeutel *Original Ditmarsch dumplings* 104
Rehrücken *Saddle of venison* 97
Reisfrikadellen *Small hamburgers with rice* 95
Rindsrouladen *Rolled stuffed steaks* 100
Rouladen *Rolled stuffed steaks* 99
Saftgulasch *Goulash* 98
Sauerbraten *Marinated beef* 93, 94
Sauerbraten Fleischklösse *Sauerbraten meatballs* 95
Sauerkraut mit Eisbein *Sauerkraut with pork hocks* 105
Sauerkraut und Schweinefleisch *Pork with sauerkraut* 105
Schlesisches Himmelreich *Silesian Heaven* 103
Schmorbraten *Braised pot roast* 98
Schwarzer Mehlbeutel *Black flour dumplings* 104
Schwarzsauer *Blacksour* 98
Semmelklösse *Bread dumplings* 102
Serviettenknödel *Napkin dumplings* 101
Spätzle *Fresh noodles* 100, 101
Steckrüben Eintopf *Turnip stew* 105
Streusel *Applecake topping* 111
Tausend Jahrs Kuchen *1,000 years cookies* 108
Uddas Ungarische Gulyassuppe *Udda's goulash soup* 91
Zwiebelkuchen *Onion cake* 86,87

SANKT MARTINSTAG *(Saint Martin's Day)*

Bettelmannpudding *Beggar's pudding* 118
Bienenstich *Honey bee cake* 127, 128
Butter oder Zuckerkuchen *Butter or sugar cake* 121
Eierscheck *Egg Custard cake* 118
Französische Windbeutel mit Vanilla Sauce *Cream puffs with vanilla sauce* 119
Gesundheitskuchen *Health cake* 125
Gewürzkuchen *Spice cake* 122
Haselnusskuchen *Hazelnut cake* 120
Haselnusstorte *Hazelnut torte* 120
Hefeteig *Yeast dough* 118
Kaffeekuchen *Coffee cake* 123, 124
Königskuchen *Royal cake* 125
Kugelhupf *Bundt cake* 126
Liegnitzer Bombe *Liegnitzer bomb* 133
Linzer Torte *Linzer torte* 134
Malakowtorte *Malakow torte* 134
Marmorgugelhupf *Marble bundt cake* 126
Mohnkuchen *Poppy seed cake* 128
Mohnstrietzel *Poppy seed cake* 130
Nussbrot *Nut bread* 130
Rehrücken Kuchen *Saddle of venison cake* 120
Rotweinkuchen *Red wine cake* 128
Schlesischer Streuselkuchen *Silesian crumb cake* 122
Schokolade Buiskuitrolle *Chocolate roll* 119
Schwarzwälderkirschtorte *Black forest cherry cake* 131, 132
Streuselkuchen *Crumb cake* 123
Zitronen Tee Brot *Lemon tea bread* 129

ADVENT, SANKT NIKOLAUS, WEIHNACHTEN
(Advent, Saint Nicholas, Christmas)

Apfel im Schlafrock *Apple in blanket* 140
Buttergebäck *Butter cookies* 145

Butterplätzchen *Butter cookies* 145
Butter Ss und Qs *Butter S's and Q's* 141
Früchtebrot *Fruit bread* 155
Gebratene Gans *Roast goose* 139
Gebratene Gans und Ente *Roast goose and duck* 140
Haselnussmakronen *Hazelnut Macaroons* 143
Heringssalat *Herring salad* 141
Johanisbeerlikör aus Schleswig-Holstein *Currant liquor from Schleswig-Holstein* 140
Knusperhäuschen *Gingerbread House* 156
Kokosmakronen *Coconut macaroons* 143
Lebkuchen *Honey spice cakes* 149
Linzer Törtchen *Linzer cookies* 142
Marzipan Pilze *Almond past mushrooms* 140
Nürnberger Elisen-Lebkuchen *Spice cakes* 148
Nüsslein *Nut cookies* 143
Springerle *Springerle* 147, 148
Spitzbuben *Little rogues* 142
Spitze Plätzchen *Lace cookies* 145
Spritzbebäck *Spritz cookies* 146, 147
Spritzgebackenes *Spritz cookies* 146
Spritz Spezialitäten *Spritz specials* 146
Weihnachtsstollen (in German and English) *Christmas Stollen* 151, 152, 153, 154
Weihnachtsstollen *Gramma's famous stollen* 154
Zimtsterne *Cinnamon stars* 144
Zitronen Herzen *Lemon hearts* 144
Zwetschgen Mänderln *Prune people* 157

INDEX
(English by category)

BREADS AND YEAST DOUGH

Bacon cake 43
Breads
    Easter bread 45
    Fruit bread 155
    Lemon tea bread 129
    Nut bread 130
Cherry souffle.......................31
Cinnamon buns 48
Doughnuts
    Fastnacht doughnuts 28
    Jelly doughnuts 28
    Mother's Berliner donuts 24
    Raisin doughnuts 29
Bavarian bread dumplings 38
Bread dumplings..................38,102
Onion cake 86, 87
Onion pie............................87
Emperor's pancakes 30
Pancakes 29
Potato pancakes 37
Rolls 46

Salt rolls 88
Christmas Stollen 151, 152, 153, 154
Stollen, Gramma's famous 154
Swabian lenten dish..................30
Yeast Braid 46
Yeast dough 118
Yeast dumplings 44

CAKES - TORTES

Apple cake 110, 111, 112, 113
Apple cake topping 111
Apple cake with crumb topping 114
Apple strudel 114
Basic cake with fruit topping 73
Bee sting cake 128
Black Forest cherry cake 131, 132
Blueberry cake 73
Brown sugar coffee cake 124
Bundt cake..........................126
Butter or sugar cake 121

Cake of the prophets 50
Cherry cake with farina 73
Cherry cake with rye bread 72
Cherry torte 72
Chocolate roll 119
Cinnamon nut coffee cake 49
Coffee cake 123, 124
Coffee ring 50
Cold dog cookie torte 109
Cottage cheese cake 76
Cottage cheese torte 77
Cream puffs with vanilla sauce 119
Crumb cake 123
Crumbs 75
Easter lamb cake 47
Egg custard cake 118
Frankfurt wreath 51
Fruit tarts 72
German coffee cake 124
Gingerbread house 156
Hazelnut cake 120
Hazelnut torte 120
Health cake 125
Hedge hog 109
Honey bee cake 127
Liegnitzer bombe 133
Linzer torte 134
Malakow torte 134
Marble bundt cake 126
Nut torte 49
Plum cake on a sheet 75
Plum tart 74
Poppy seed cake 128, 130
Red wine cake 128
Refrigerator cheese cake 76
Rhubarb pie 74
Royal cake 125
Saddle of venison cake 120
Silesian crumb cake 122
Spice cake 122
Sponge cake for torte 75
Strawberry blitz torte 69
Tree cake 50
Wood shavings or wheel cakes 109

COOKIES

Butter cookies 145
Butter S's and Q's 141
Cinnamon stars 144
Coconut macaroons 143
Cookie press cookies 146, 147
Hazelnut macaroons 143
Honey spice cakes 149
Lace cookies 145
Linzer cookies 142
Little rogues 142
Lemon hearts 144
Nut cookies 143

Old fashion German vanilla cookies 108
1,000 years cookies 108
Spice cakes 148
Springerle 147, 148
Spritz cookies 146
Spritz specials 146

DESSERTS

Apple in blanket 140
Beggar's pudding 118
Dessert apple fritters 115
Dish pleasing to the gods 25
Farina pudding 81
Lemon creme 79
Red fruit pudding 80
Rhubarb souffle 80
Rum-laced stew plums 80
Steamed pudding 107
Stewed rhubarb 81

FISH

Blue trout 44

MEATS

Beefsteak Tartar 17
Blacksour 98
Braised beef rolls 99
Braised pot roast 98
Chicken fricassee 62
Chicken-veal fricassee 61
Cold cut platter 18
Fried calves liver 63
Fried liver with onions and apples ... 63
German meatballs with sour cream 66
Goulash 98
Hamburgers with rice 95
Ham filled pockets 62
Ham noodle souffle 70, 71
Helga's hash 68
Homemade sausage 107
Hot liver pâté 92
Hunter's veal cutlet 97
Liver dumplings 64
Marinated beef 93, 94
Marinated roast (Easy) 94
Marinated pot roast 93
Marinated roast 94
Meatballs, Königsberg style 65, 66
Meatballs in caper sauce 64
Meat filled noodles 61
Pork hocks with sauerkraut 105
Pork loin 99
Pork with sauerkraut 105
Pot pie 96
Rabbit stew 96
Roasted tame rabbit 96
Roast goose 139
Roast goose and duck 140

Rolled stuffed steaks 99, 100
Saddle of venison 97
Sailor's hash 68
Sauerbraten meatballs 95
Sausage loaf 106
Silesian heaven 103
Steak 22
Stew 69
Stuffed cucumbers 106
Tartar 17
Tasty sliced tongue 18
Turnip stew 105
Veal fricassee 62

MISCELLANEOUS

Almond paste mushrooms 140
Assorted cheese appetizers 19
Camembert spread 107
Easter pretzels 46
Good luck mushroom men 20
Ham toast - Hawaii style 19
Prune people 157
Quick cheese appetizers 88

POTATO AND NOODLE DISHES

Black flour dumplings 104
Cottage cheese plum dumplings 33
Ditmarscher dumplings 104
Dried fruit and dumplings 103
Dumplings 23, 104
Egg dumplings 31
Farmer's breakfast 45
Filled noodles 32
Fresh noodles 100, 101
Heaven and earth 64
Home fries 106
Napkin dumplings 101
Potato dumplings 23, 102
Raw potato dumplings 24
Steamed sweet dumplings 34, 35, 36

PUNCH - BEVERAGES

Elite artillery punch 15
Currant liquor 140
Eggnog 15
Fire tong or rum punch 14
Peach punch 82
Punch for cold evenings 16
Rum and fruit crock 81
Spiced wine 15

SALADS

Bavarian cabbage salad 56
Boston lettuce 70, 71
Celeriac salad 56

Cucumber boats 21
Herring salad 17, 141
Meat salad, cooked 18
Potato salad 16, 56
Prinkenauer potato salad 57
Red beet eggs 20
Russian eggs 20
Wurst salad 19

SAUCES

Green sauce 43
Rhine sauce 55
Seven spoon sauce 55
Sweet and sour sauce for salads 55
Vanilla creme 78
Vanilla sauce 33, 78
Wine creme 78
Wine sauce 79

SOUPS

Asparagus soup 57
Cabbage soup 89
Farina or cream of wheat soup 38
Fresh soup with dumplings 91
Goulash soup 92
Lentil soup 22
Liver dumpling soup 88
Marrow dumpling soup 89
Pancake soup 39
Potato soup 89, 90
Soup with pancake strips 39
Sour cherry soup 58
Sour lentils with noodles 21
Split pea soup 90
Split pea soup with knockwurst 90
Udda's goulash soup 91

VEGETABLES

Asparagus toast Daniel 57
Cabbage strudel 60
Hot celeriac 56
Mixed vegetables a la Leipzig 59
Paradise cabbage 55
Red cabbage 58
Spinach and eggs 43
Stuffed cabbage rolls 60
Sweet-sour cabbage 55
Vegetable chowder 59

NOTES

NOTES

NOTES